S H A
R A

MAKING A
Pearl
FROM THE
Grit
OF LIFE

pinctada
publishing

Making a Pearl from the Grit of Life / by Sharon E. Rainey

ISBN 978-0-615-38613-3

Developed by Ascent, a Division of Hazard Communications, Inc.,
PO Box 6132, Leesburg, VA 20132

Cover & Interior: Lookout Design, Inc.

Printed by Dickinson Press, Grand Rapids, Michigan

pinctada
publishing
Pinctada Publishing
1146-D Walker Road
Great Falls, VA 22066
www.pinctadapublishing.com

First printing October 2010

I do not choose my stories; they choose me.
They demand to be told.

NATALIE GOLDBERG, JULY, 2008
TAOS SUMMER WRITER'S CONFERENCE

To Karen,
may you make
many pearls!

For Jeffrey
who always tells me the truth

For Stephen
whose story is the first one I gained the courage to tell

I Am From

I am from Earle who was "Son" or "Brother"
and from June who was born in May.
I am from a steamy summer night in Birmingham, Alabama.

I am from Nora & Henry Earle and Charles & Flo.

I am from the heat of Marengo County, Alabama,
the Blue Ridge Mountains of Keyser, West Virginia.

I am from the Texas sun, desert, and mountains
that end only at the Earth's edge.

I am from a purgatory of wooded
northern Virginia suburbia where
power is at its pinnacle.

I am from sweet tea, baked cod, steak on Sunday,
and green beans cooked for an hour.

I am from educators, seamstresses, china
painters, sheep herders, and store owners.

I am from four generations of college-educated women.

I am from silence, secret keepers and Ya-Ya sisters.

I am from obligation, honor and integrity.

I am from nest builders, homemakers, and caregivers.

I am from
"Do the Right Thing,"
"You must always do your best,"
"Your word is your bond," and
"Children should be seen and not heard."

I am from Dag Nab It.

I am from Presbyterians and Methodists
depending on which side of town you live on.

I am from desert sand and grit;
imperfect
I am from God's eyes and God's heart;
perfect in my human-ness.

A Word Before

*All sorrows can be borne if you put them into a story
or tell a story about them.— Isak Dinesen*

"Life is messy."

Three times in less than five hours I heard this statement from random, unrelated, people. I had just presented a rough draft of my 'memoir' at a writers' conference in Taos, New Mexico. In minutes, my dream of being a published author was crushed by eleven women. And within the critique of my manuscript, my instructor wrote, "Life is messy. You cannot always put order into a person's life and make it all nice and neat. It just doesn't work that way."

These words settled like a grain of coarse sand inside my hopeful, tender soul.

After class, I called my husband, Jeff, so he could tell me how wrong they were. "You know, babe, sometimes life is messy. And you can't always live in a perfectly organized time-line. You may just need to go outside the box on this one." Life is messy. I did not tell him that he had just uttered the words that set my teeth on edge just hours before.

Later, I sat in the rented Dodge Santa Fe, wiping my tears on my shirt. I prayed, thinking, first, it might help me feel better and, second, it might look good in front of God and He might grant my request for an easy road to publishing my work.

Remember the joke, "Want to make God laugh? Tell him your plans." I think God was chuckling at that moment. But also, as He has done many times, He was also carefully, gently, preparing a small message to ease the hurt.

I prayed more and asked God for guidance, for a sign, a light to show me the next step.

I headed to my lonely dinner for one at the Guacamole Grill. While waiting for an opening in traffic, I glanced across the main road to the top of the San Christo Mountain's mottled, kelly-green and gray forest. Down-slope from the peaks, the sun's rays were moving over the hills, striking the lower part of range full-strength, turning its tree stands a radiant lime green. . . unfolding a path of light as slowly progressed.

The message to me: *I do not need to see the final destination; I just need to know what my next move is.*

Healing words, poured over my bitter disappointment.

Still. I nursed the wound a little longer. Felt the sharp edges of the gritty rejection. Why could I not let the harsh words of a small handful of people go?

I ate outside, journaling about the painful afternoon, questioning if I needed to change the focus of my intended project. I paused, looked up; a rainbow traversed the mountain directly in front of me. Where was the spooky music? This was getting weird. I wrote another page in my journal and looked up again to see a double rainbow. I heard the couple at the table next to me admiring this remarkable event of nature. *Relax. Like any other aspect of Creation, do your own task, and allow those who have the eyes to see find and be moved by your simple words.*

Message received. Reluctantly.

I drove back to my isolated *casita* on the plateau, still miffed… at God or everyone, who knows?—but grateful for a solitary respite. Still feeling rebellious, still wanting full critical approbation from my erudite colleagues, I turned on the television. The 19" box had remained silent all week—a gift to myself—a quiet and insulated time from the rest of the world. But tonight, I would show my classmates . . . I would do the forbidden thing and watch TV, just to *show them*.

"House, MD" blinked on. Greg House, the brilliant, funny, obnoxious, drug-addicted diagnostician played by actor Hugh Laurie, said, "You know, sometimes life is messy."

A messy life, rainbows, and prayer are what helped get me through the development of this book—just as a difficult path, sudden signs, and—especially—moments when my soul has been opened (despite my efforts to stay closed and grasping to what I want) by the actions of a force outside myself, allowing wisdom and guidance for the next step to flood in and form what has become my life. My life in spite of *me*.

My faith, family and friends are the key elements throughout. I'm not 'different' from anyone else. Crises and tough emotional periods are the grit around which my inner self has been formed. Some, I have come through with more grace than others. But with each challenging situation, each nightmare— each new piece of grit embraced and transformed—I came through with a more loving family, deeper friendships, and an even more profound relationship with God.

Perhaps it's because I am a former teacher that I have always, at least, recognized when I am being presented with opportunities to learn new lessons (do they have to be presented so continuously?). Sometimes the lesson is not to accept unacceptable behavior; or to be patient and tolerant; to accept the waiting periods of my life. At other times, the lesson has been larger; the most important ones being about forgiveness. At age 47, I am still realizing that happiness only truly comes from that great 'letting go' of our insistence that life and the people in our life be *exactly* what we want them to be—the letting go we can only refer to as the grace of forgiveness.

I have found forgiveness to be a messy process only because of my own restrictions, inherited beliefs, and self-doubt. I have had to let go of all self-limiting thoughts before I could finally create a place in my heart that is able to commit a simple, clear act of forgiveness. Clearing out all negative "stuff," I have come to create a place in my heart of serenity, acceptance, beauty, balance, and love.

With each opportunity before me, God presented me with a choice. I could accept His offerings, His wisdom, His grace. Or I could choose to hold onto the pain, the anger and the resentment a little longer. I resisted letting go. As I held on, God waited. An opportunity to learn the very same lesson presented itself later.

I had to clear up my messy life. By letting go of the debris and filth, I have come to a deeper, more soulful beauty and clarity like an oasis in the desert. From that place of clarity, a vision of what I could have, what I could do, who I could be has emerged if I allow my heart to become a place of compassion, acceptance and forgiveness.

It was in letting go and receiving these graces that the very things that had just been grit were transformed into pearls... and now offered here in this writing as a gift of enduring, unconditional love.

But what I'm telling you now is a great life lesson learned through a long, long process. The process of my life so far. This book is not a memoir; it is not an autobiography. It is a book about healing.

Life is messy. Grit and grace come at us fast, side by side. Sometimes the grit becomes overwhelming and diminishes our spirit. What's good seems lost and gone forever. This is a story about the pathway back to what's beautiful, when the way back seems impossible.

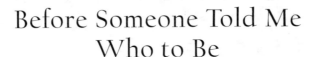

Before Someone Told Me
Who to Be

"To thine own self be true."—*William Shakespeare*

"Who were you before someone else told you who to be?"

I was 45 when a writing instructor asked this question in a class setting. Even though I was sitting still in a chair, I felt like Wylie Coyote, tied to the end of the boulder that he pushes over the cliff edge, hoping it will land on the roadrunner. As Wylie pushes the boulder over and realizes that he will be going in the same direction, his feet push as hard as they can against the ground, hoping that magically, he will not end up where the boulder ends up. And yet, that's exactly where Wylie ended up. That is where I ended up, figuratively, dragged into a buried memory that surfaced only at that very moment.

That memory opened me, and allowed me to discover my spiritual core.

El Paso, Texas, 1968; the southwestern desert. I am five years old. I am playing outside with my across the street neighbor and best friend, Christy, riding my bike up and down our street, venturing to 7-Eleven for a 10-cent Hershey chocolate bar. Getting there is uphill a bit; I have to pedal hard. As usual,

I am barefoot with my Keds in the basket attached to the handlebars. Calluses have toughened my soles so gripping the foot pedals is easy. The Keds are just protection from the hot pavement. My daily play uniform is my bathing suit or shorts and a sleeveless shirt.

Though I know what I am going to buy, I stand in front of the candy section for a long time, inspecting each type to see if it is something new, something I might like to try. But, I only have a dime, and I am unwilling to risk of trying something I might not like. Nope, Hershey's chocolate is the best bet.

For most months of the year, Christy and I pedal two-tenths of a mile from our house to the pool for a day of swimming and sometimes floating in the chilled water. My favorite part of floating is that for those few moments, I am weightless, directionless, and silent. I close my eyes, feeling the sun's rays dry my front side, warming it to the day's temperature while beneath the water my back remains cool. I can only float on the quieter days, though; when not so many kids are kicking and splashing. On the more crowded days we play shark with the older kids who always tag us first.

The return trip is faster and easier, mostly downhill. This is the simple cycle of my life, and this memory is smooth, like a gently rolling landscape with few remarkable features: I could be writing about any one of a thousand days.

There came one day that was chillier than most. It is vivid as the present:

The ride home from 7-Eleven is cooler. My legs are longer than Christy's, affording me a stronger cycling motion on my bigger bike. Christy is still too short for a big person's bike; instead, she shows off with her banana seat and wide handle bars, red pom-pom tassels hanging from each.

I can't see my shadow in the street; the sun has disappeared behind a strange grey cloud. I am pedaling so quickly the breeze has chilled my ears. I notice small, white raindrops polka-dotting my arms, my thighs, the sidewalk in front and the grass beside me. They drop slowly, like the beginning of a rainstorm that lingers for awhile; but doesn't leave much in the way of water. These drops are colder than rain, and prettier. I look around; the polka-dots fall on the roofs of the houses, too, and then disappear as well.

And then—the split-second transition from question to epiphany.

"Snow!" Christy and I yell, simultaneously. We have never seen real snow before, except in picture books and national weather forecasts.

It is like the moment when water pours from the pump into Helen Keller's hands. Sheer, visceral ecstasy floods my body in this instant of connection.

I drop my bike onto the grass, running in the grass, sleeve-less arms outstretched. The cold droplets melt as quickly as I can capture their unique shapes and designs. Their trickles still give me goose bumps. My towhead pigtails disguise the flakes but they dapple Christy's strawberry blond hair with more white polka dots.

Instinctively, I keep my face pointed to the sky, holding out my tongue, catching the confetti as it falls. Bewilderment, fascination, joy; all three emotions experienced within nano-seconds of one another. It is happening too fast!

As instantly as it began, the snow ends—but not before imprinting a memory tableau in my brain; a single moment when my young soul is fully revealed.

Who was I before someone else told me who to be?

I was a happy, wandering, playful little girl, amazed by the unexplainable, excited by new discoveries, embracing experiences, accepting glorious gifts, and grateful to be the chosen recipient of it all.

Soon after, other voices started telling me who to be. It has taken a journey of forty years to rediscover this wondrous child. Now, I hold her close every day, doing my best to honor her for all she was, is, and hopes to be.

Memories and Dreams

Memories are the key not to the past,
but to the future.—Corrie Ten Boom

I have many happy memories of my life in El Paso. I lived there until I was seven. I remember the ever-present bright sunlight, bike rides for chocolate bars, playing Marco Polo at the pool, squeals of delight with my best friend Christy, sunshine warming my skin. My only boundaries were how far I could ride my bike. Though my world was really only a half-mile radius from the house, my boundaries were limitless since the sky never stopped; desert mountains decorated horizons.

At night, I dreamt of flying. I flew upwards, forwards, drifted in circles, and soared through the clouds. All of my dreams were intense, vivid, powerful. I rocketed from the ground into the clouds' linings, coming to a gentle coast, drifting in and out, above and below the shape changing cotton balls. I flew where the snowflakes formed and danced by their side as they drifted downward. As they touched the ground, I always jettisoned again before my heels settled against the earth.

There was nothing but pure being.

I floated among the clouds in my favorite dreams, not necessarily with any direction, but always knowing I would not fall; I commanded how high, how fast, and how far my body traveled. I didn't see anyone else in my dreams, yet I never felt alone. I always felt protected, almost giddy with glee. I adventured to wonderful worlds that reached far beyond where I could ever walk. They were there; just waiting for me to leap.

White Sands

Laughter is soul making, too.
No matter how dark and serious a crisis seems,
I shouldn't abandon my joy.—Sue Monk Kidd

Being outside in warm sunshine with no physical boundaries was my sanctuary. In wide-open spaces I could be whomever and whatever I wanted to be. My dreams were as limitless as my surroundings. The outdoor sounds echoed with me, shouting back at me, "You are real. And you have a place in this world." I was fully alive, an element of the scene, acknowledged by nature. A simple recognition of my presence: sunburn or a bug bite. The deeper validation came internally with exhilarating emotions of pure, simple joy.

Not only a delightful sense of being, but validation that came from starkly beautiful places.

White Sands, New Mexico is the location of the first atomic bomb test in 1945. A portion of it has remained a military test site. In the 1960s, my father's company worked with the military, participating in the research at White Sands. On occasion, my family accompanied Dad on the trip. Mom dropped him off at the entrance to the base; then took us to the National Monument site where we played for hours and picnicked until Dad's work was done.

My memory of this particular visit is almost miniscule, fragmented into separated picture frames, eventually developing into a flip-book. I remember my two older sisters, Gayle and Carol, rolling down endless mountains of white sand with me, each mountain at least 20 feet high. Climbing back up the massive mounds of sand, my feet slid with each step. My hair, the same ecru as these hills, blew about, my sand-covered hands trying to clear my view, trying to avoid getting the grains into my eyes.

My breath quickened and deepened with each step to the summit. The sun had warmed the sand's top layer. But as my toes dug under, the cool grains tickled between my toes. The Organ Mountain range shadowed the perimeter more as host than boundary. The sun's reflection off the white floor blinded me as I looked up, tears watering my eyes. It was much easier to look down, at the end goal and starting point, all in one.

I laughed as I climbed in expectation of the coming delight. I laughed as I rolled like a barrel down the slopes, arms crossed against my chest, my hair tangling with the sand.

My mother also joyfully laughed as all three daughters repeatedly rolled down and climbed back up. I glimpsed her outline with the sun behind, casting her long shadow in the sand. I caught her smile, like an instamatic camera, her own sand-covered hands trying to brush away her not so naturally coal black hair from her eyes. Most of all, I remember her here, laughing. It filled my ears. Her smile, her sparkling eyes, and her infectious laughter, along with the vistas, were limitless and unending and powerful.

Her sandy fingers pulled my hair into a ponytail. Her shadow cooled my feet. The gritty white dunes, the invigorating sun, and my mother's laughter told me that I was loved.

At White Sands, I could see it and feel it and know it. As tangible as the first snowdrops landing on my arms, I felt my mother's love and acceptance of me; something that most children take for granted, but as an adult, I am grateful for.

Conforming

The past affects the present even without our
being aware of it.—Francine Shapiro

In El Paso, the walk to school was only two-tenths of a mile from my house, but it was beyond the end of my street, and thus, a tiny adventure twice a day walking to and fro with my sister Carol.

I remember only fragments of my kindergarten year: finger painting on colored construction paper and rest time on squeaky plastic mats with closed venetian blinds, and racing for the swings at recess. At the top of the classroom's blackboard, each member of the alphabet was written as a capital letter and small letter. Day by day, each letter became a new set of lines on the map of meaning.

I experienced some typical childhood teasing. I was the only kindergartener with glasses. A sign of the times: they were cat-eye shaped. Even today, I cringe at my school photos wondering how in the world I could have chosen them. But I did. And my classmates quickly named me "four eyes."

I was also different from the other students because I did not eat lunch in the cafeteria. Each day, I walked the two-tenths of a mile home to eat Kraft Macaroni & Cheese, my favorite dish. I had developed a stomach ulcer at a very young age, reason unknown. In the 1960s, physicians thought these ulcers were caused by worry and cured by coating the stomach. My diet was severely restricted. I drank lukewarm milk every two hours and ate bland foods followed by two chalky Mylanta tablets. I had to chew each bite 30 times to make sure it was easily digestible. Most of the time, I was allowed only plain pasta. When I graduated to pasta with butter, life was looking mighty good. So I ate the mac and cheese, drank my milk, choked down the Mylanta tablets, and walked back to school in time for afternoon class.

In first grade, I received my first real storybook; level one of the McKee Reader books. The cover had a Christmas green background with a mischievous looking spaniel puppy dog on the front. He had a green collar on that made his head and his body sort of look separated from each other. In his mouth, he was carrying a rag-doll doubling as the joker in a deck of cards.

Eagerly, Mrs. Fugate asked us to say the name of the book out loud. Hurriedly, before my classmates, bouncing up from the reading circle, I shouted, "TYPE!" With a pause and giggles and a snicker or two, my classmates shouted back, "TIP!" In the other books I had read, I knew the words. I could pronounce them and knew their meaning. But this was one word I did not know. And now everyone else knew, as well, that I did not know it.

In a single instant, a strong but subtle sense began to take hold—my sense of being separate and unlike my peers. In this instance, and later in others, when I made a mistake, classmates laughed and taunted me. And so a feeling began to grow inside—a feeling that was uncomfortable, like a grain or coarse grit deep inside my soul. I was defective, somehow just always . . . wrong.

I liked my life better when there was no school, no rules, no competition, no failures. When there was no school, I could play and dream, and be whomever and whatever I wanted to be. When there was no school, there were no limits, no shame, no harm.

Within just the first few months of my education, one of my earliest life lessons had just been branded onto me. I learned early and quickly to remain quiet among my peers until I *knew* my answers were accurate or otherwise, face humiliation, followed by shunning.

Fortunately, my teachers didn't offer a form of rescue. Rather, they showed me how to work through the mistakes and keep moving forward. From then on, my eyes always focused forward, ignoring the kids around me. I focused on pleasing the teacher; doing anything to impress or gain acceptance. I learned that if my peers were going to push me away, I would just stuff the feelings of rejection and separation. I would try to be more perfect on the outside.

Terrified of being forgotten or cast away, I learned once again to attract attention through positive actions, intriguing discussions, and willingness. By first grade, my sense of worth was in direct proportion to what I learned and what I contributed back to the class.

I had already become a human *doing* instead of a human *being*.

Moving Silence

The silence is as important as the noise. What gets left out is as important as what gets included.—Sara Lawrence-Lightfoot

I do believe that I had to experience every part of my life so that I can be where I am now. But I still have the "what ifs" about some of those events. In 1970, after I finished first grade, my family moved from the beautiful grand expanse of the southwestern desert to evergreen trees and four seasons of Northern Virginia. At age 7, I was excited about this new adventure; completely unaware of the pervasive wallop and extensive changes it would make in my life down to the cellular level.

We flew to Virginia on July 1st.

Peering out of the plexi-glass window, I saw soft, miniature bubbles popping out of the ground, the Blue Ridge Mountains. They were my first glance at the new land.

These mounds were nothing like the sharp-edged jagged mountains of the southwest. Each of these bubbles was green; or green with brown; or brown with green, or really dark green. Even with the sun shining on them, I couldn't find anything that wasn't moiled green or brown. In Texas, when the sun hit the mountains, they transformed from one color to all different colors of the rainbow, depending on the season and the day's weather.

The river beyond the mountains was brown. Water isn't brown . . . .

"Why is the water brown?" I wondered.

As the plane headed away from the mountains, patch-works of green and yellow squares blanketed the flatter sur-faces where farmers alternated crops. The barns next to the fields were larger than the houses alongside them. And the round things . . . I learned later they were called silos.

This land came with its own vocabulary. Sitting on the other side of the plane, my two sisters only occasionally glanced out the window. Was their world looking and feeling as different as mine? It didn't seem to bother them or affect them as it did me. Everyone else seemed to already know the answers, so I thought I was supposed to already know them as well.

I started seeing roads, tall buildings and houses, all of them grouped together, overlapped with tall green trees. Each group was put close together—crowded. This was very differ-ent from the open expanses of Texas. I just didn't know how to integrate the new colors, shapes, and dimensions.

The suffocating Virginia summer heat attached to my skin like seaweed as we moved from the plane to the people mov-ers. It staled the air; wet, heavy, coating my arms and legs, fill-ing my nose with a mixture of jet engine fuel and sweat. I felt five pounds heavier with what I could only understand as dirt. I didn't know what humidity was; but I knew what it felt like. I knew what it smelled like, and how it oppressed my lungs.

Nausea built up in my stomach as if I was suddenly on a rocking boat trying to establish some solid grounding under my feet. The landscape didn't match and the colors definitely didn't correspond.

I left a limitless world and entered a strange land concealed by gigantic, invasive plants and suffocating heavy air. The sky was still blue, but the world seemed darker, the sun blocked where the trees stood, caging my world.

I felt disconnected, different, and alone.

This is where life as I knew it changed. This is where a new feeling slowly, eventually, permeated every cell of my body, changing the way I took in the world. My perceptions, opinions, everything changed the year I moved from Texas to Virginia.

The next part of my story is difficult for me to recall; not because the memories are fuzzy, but because it is painful for me to remember that five year old child who had been so happy, so filled with dreams and hope... and then to watch that child change into a depressed, lonely soul.

I issue a formal disclaimer: For some, alienation comes from living in deprived and difficult circumstances; I was not raised in any sort of deprived, unhealthy manner. My parents were middle class; they owned the homes where we lived. They put me in Girl Scouts, provided me with sewing classes, horseback riding lessons, and anything else I wanted. They taught me what parents are 'supposed' to teach their children. They told me and showed me they loved me. They paid for my college degrees. I do not, in any way, blame them for the difficulties I experienced in my childhood. Their presence in my life was and is essential, a force for the good.

It was that tiny grain of grit—not the white sand of beautiful New Mexico, but the grit of shame—that remained deep in my being, and slowly, slowly over time its effects would spread to every cell in my body. It would completely alter me; it would change everything. It would twist its shape and become a disease; its name was depression.

When we arrived in Virginia, our home was not yet completed, so we stayed in a rental home for six months on a crowded *cul-de-sac*, mostly Colonial-style homes sliced into tiny rooms with even tinier windows. The forest surrounded each house, including ours; just a 15-foot perimeter of grass. Gargantuan trees draped over the Monopoly square houses. More skyscraper trees filled the front yards forbidding kickball or tag. I rode my bike up and down the *cul-de-sac* and the single adjoining street. If they see me they'll come out to play. I don't remember anyone coming to play or ride or even to say hi. The outdoors had become a world of silence and invisibility.

The pool was more than a half-mile away; the ride there completely downhill which meant coming home was a short ride and a long walk alongside my bike uphill for the remainder. Alone. It wasn't like the hill to 7-Eleven in El Paso; this one was impossible to climb even with my legs another year longer and stronger. But more importantly, there were no desert vistas or mountains.

September. I stood alone at a bus stop slightly apart from the same kids who never came out to play; another piece of the new world's boundaries and restrictions. They talked and giggled together. Sometimes, they asked me a question; when I replied, they turned to each other knowingly and laughed again. The families with kids my age were Catholic or Jewish, neither of which I had heard of until Virginia.

No one gave me the secret decoder ring on how to make friends. In El Paso, Christy had just been there, living across the street. I don't remember the first time we met; we had always played together. Kids were always at the pool and we had fun in the water. It wasn't work; it was friendship. And it just sort of happened. Here in Virginia friendships did not just "happen." And I didn't understand why.

That fall, I remember visiting one neighborhood girl my age at the other end of the street. In her bedroom, the cross above her headboard had Jesus hanging on it. It was the first time I ever saw a crucifix. It terrified me. How in the world could anyone sleep with Jesus suffering in agony right above? In a childish way, I became grateful for being a Presbyterian. I couldn't fathom going to church every Sunday and seeing nothing but Christ's suffering. It was easier this way for me to develop my relationship with God. I knew Christ suffered and died for me, but that wasn't the focus of church for me. A plain cross was enough to focus my thoughts on the minister's message. It allowed me to hear more clearly and thus feel more deeply the message of God's love for me.

There was no Presbyterian church in my town, so we attended one in a different town twenty minutes away. None of my classmates went to my church. I didn't know these other kids in this other church; they all went to school together in this other town. My neighbors all went to church or temple together. It was another disconnect.

For seven years in the desert, the outdoors accepted me and connected me with other kids my age. I was a part of the group, of the excitement and adventure, of happiness. In Virginia, acceptance and community with my peers were the exception rather than the rule.

When we moved into our new home, I finally had a room to myself, 8'x9' with robin's egg blue walls. It was large enough to fit a twin bed and a small dresser. I loved not having to share with my sisters, but, looking back now, I see that my four walls isolated me even more, including from my family.

I never learned how to speak, how to communicate, how to describe my feelings of isolation, aloneness, of unhappiness. I did the only thing I knew how to do: I built my own walls of silence to disguise my desperation and what later came to be recognized and diagnosed as depression. I stopped talking—not completely, like becoming mute, but I just stopped conversing, integrating, connecting. I thought by masking the depression with silence, the feelings might disappear.

I was too young to realize the impact of my decisions; my separation and aloneness took me closer and closer to hitting a bottom. I thought everyone would still see me through my walls and wonder what the big mess was on the other side. What I didn't realize was that I had created strong, impenetrable, opaque walls. It was as if I had adorned myself with an invisibility cloak that no one noticed as they passed by.

I realize now that I was desperately searching for a place of safety; a refuge from the world. I wanted to return to my limitless vistas, never-ending sunshine, and easy bike-pedaling hills. I found no safety in the Virginia evergreens. What I found was that when something destroys that sense of safety, an opening occurs in the soul of the child who feels the great distance between happiness and unhappiness, love and pain. And into that deep, deep opening—which we minimize by calling insecurity—will fall the painful grains of life's grit. And without graces of love, forgiveness, those painful grains will work their way deeper....

Toughen Up

The echo of one of God's deepest truths: delight can emerge from and exist along with our scars.—Sue Monk Kidd

By third grade, I focused my energy on learning cursive and multiplication tables, working again to please the teachers and grateful to have women constantly praising my efforts. I was hungry for attention and relationships.

Winter in Virginia held gray skies, impenetrable clouds (even in my dreams), and snow, from November 15th until April 1st. My body craved sunshine; winter felt like an addict's withdrawal.

In the 1970s, no one talked about depression or Seasonal Affective Disorder; in children, it wasn't even acknowledged. It certainly wasn't seen as normal. But when I moved to Virginia, this weird, horrible dread took control of my mind and my body and never seemed to let go. The darkness was there whether the sun was shining or hiding behind the hideous winter clouds.

I remember thinking I wanted to die rather than live through another February day of grayness; I didn't tell anyone because I knew it wasn't normal. And normal was all I ever wanted to be.

Why did I want to die? Because living was just so damn hard, even at age 10. When all I had to do was get up in the morning and go to school, it was more than drudgery; it was excruciating. Every day was a reinforcement of all I didn't have: connections to life—no friends, no sleepovers, no mid-class giggles or note passing.

The only attention I attracted at school was from a '50s-looking nerd named Myron. Every day, every time he passed by me, he pulled my bra-strap and snapped it like a slingshot, stinging my back. At the time, I was the only girl in the class wearing a bra. I yelped from the pain as much as the surprise, arching my back in a fruitless attempt to lessen both. Myron would smile through his nerdy glasses, sticking his hands in his black high-water pants as he passed by.

When I complained to the teacher, she half-heartedly admonished him, knowing the pleas only magnified his behavior. At least Mrs. Curtis' discipline was an acknowledgement of the wrongfulness. At least someone was telling him to stop.

"Just ignore him; eventually he will stop." I tried it for two weeks. He didn't stop. Mrs. Curtis' admonishments became an "evil eye" glare of silence; which had the same effect as her words: nothing. Myron snapped my bra-strap at least once every day for the entire year of fourth grade.

When the next September arrived, I was no longer the only girl wearing a bra and Myron had moved.

Throughout my life, others have suggested that I "toughen up." This incident was the first time I heard that suggestion. I was ten years old. I didn't know what it meant. I felt as though I was being attacked. I wanted someone to acknowledge me and fight for me.

I am, by God's design, a "feeler." Everything in the world I interpret with my feelings. I am hyper-sensitive to others' hurtful words. I find it almost impossible to let what others say "*just* roll off my back." I personalize too much of what anyone says to me. This is definitely not a good characteristic, but it is how God created me. I have worked very hard through the years to change this, with very little success.

Some people have stated it is one of my greatest character defects while others have lauded it as a great strength that has enabled me to develop a deep empathy for others who suffer in life. Personally, it is a burden to feel so hurt by others' words, though it has caused me to be a more open and compassionate human being.

Looking back now at my ten-year-old self, unprepared to stand and fight for myself, I see the path I had angled off on: the path of inner isolation. I was left to interpret life and its meanings on my own. And with my hypersensitivity, the signals that came in seemed to say I wasn't worth other people's time, attention, or praise.

The Big Time

Until we heal the child we used to be, the adult we want to be doesn't stand a chance.—Marianne Williamson

After my embarrassing reading circle moment in first grade when I had pronounced the book title as Type instead of Tip, I withdrew from class participation. One of the gifts of the Virginia elementary schools was an open classroom environment allowing students to learn at their own pace. I thrived in this system, loving the individuality and solitude it offered. I worked alone, succeeding in academics and not worrying about the friendships I didn't have.

I survived Myron's bra strap snapping and teasing. I walked laps around the field rather than be picked last for kickball. Feeling betrayed already by my peers, instead I made friends with my teachers and asked for more homework. Yep, I was a nerd, the teacher's pet. I was ecstatic when my sixth grade teacher Miss Fisher handed us *One Day in the Life of Ivan Denisovich,* by Alexander Solzhenitsyn for our class reading assignment (I still have my copy). I was mesmerized by his abundant, rich description of such austere, hopeless moments. While my days of angst were miniscule compared to Solzhenitsyn's experience, I identified with the feelings. Out of that book, my hope flourished that someday life would get better. I would escape the darkness.

As is true for most teenagers, seventh and eighth grades were two terrible years, filled with rumor mills, a two-timing first boyfriend, slam books, and a best friend who dumped me. I recently found a box of her letters and notes to me. Her reasons for ending the friendship are still as vague to me today as they were then. Now, though, I can chuckle at the absurdity and cliché:

> **"As far as our friendship is, there really isn't one.** I don't want to walk away, but you and I will never get along."

Six months later, she wrote:

> **"We came to a fork in the road which made it necessary for us to go our separate ways.** We changed and didn't fulfill each other's needs. Or maybe it was we just didn't need each other."

She must have been reading Robert Frost. I can still envision the long-haired blonde dramatically acting the drama out with her arms outstretched; her face exaggerated with emotion.

Ages 12 to 14 simply suck. But at the time, I didn't know my peers were having their own crises. No one was showing me theirs. It wasn't a Facebook world yet. I only knew of my own inner suffering.

Yes, there were times—days and moments—when I was laughing, enjoying my friends, going ice skating, wishing "he" would ask me to dance when the deejay dimmed the lights, started the disco ball and played "Color My World" by Chicago.

But for some unfathomable reason, my childhood was molded, darkened by a continuously growing sense of inexplicable hopelessness.

I didn't call it depression. I just knew I was incredibly sad for no discernable reason. While rain tended to exacerbate the darkness within, I could feel the same thing on a summer day. It didn't matter if great things or horrible things had happened through the day. There seemed to be no rhyme or reason to my emotions. Sometimes I would be fine; and some weeks I was sad, hopeless, lethargic, wishing I could just stay in my bed until the feeling left me. My black hole was deepening; my airway, my throat, my voice continued constricting.

At age 15, I thought my life was taking a turn towards the light. Maybe the darkness was lifting. I became a sophomore at a new local high school, just opening its doors with no junior or senior class. I was suddenly top dog, in the Big Time.

School was 20 minutes closer, twice as small. Students were brought in from three nearby high schools, which meant opportunities for new friendships and cream-of-the-crop teachers from all across the county.

I was selected as co-editor of the school newspaper. This single event brought my first opportunity to find my voice with a gifted teacher/writer/reporter who loved his job(s), respected his students, and became my favorite teacher of all time. He taught me how to write a five-paragraph essay. He was a funny storyteller, injecting humor into each class lesson. He taught us grammar through writing, something unheard of for that decade. He taught me how to appreciate and respect a piece of literature without necessarily liking it.

He supervised the newspaper content and production without micro-managing it. In our first year, we placed first in the state's annual high school journalism competition.

But even as the school year progressed, amidst academic progress and opportunity, of developing talent and increased acknowledgement, of a burgeoning voice, my perspective dimmed anything positive. I started again to feel I was drowning in those damned depressive episodes, which lasted for days; and sometimes, months.

Four Bottles

Depression is a disease. It can kill you.—*Lee Frazier*

I was determined to succeed in my effort with no one knowing ahead of time. My actions were clear and decisive. Of course, they would all know when it was over, but in order for it to work, for now, total secrecy was essential. If one other person knew before completion, my plan would fail. I began my preparation immediately following a surprise 16th birthday party my friends had given me.

The night of my party, I thought I was going ice-skating, my outfit was nothing particularly special. We stopped at a friend's house to pick her up, but we actually reached the destination for what I now realized was a party for me!

What started out as surprising and exciting finished as a typical teenage drama. A friend of mine invited a boy whom she had a crush on. By the end of the evening, this boy, in her opinion, paid too much attention to me and not enough to her. He asked me to slow dance; he brought me a plate of chips and snacks; and he offered to drive me home. The celebration that started with squeals and laughter ended with scowls and tense silence regardless of the fact that I had no say in who was invited and needed a ride home since no one had planned that far for me, including my parents. Everyone who had started the party wishing me a Happy Birthday now left without acknowledging my presence or the purpose of the event.

The birthday party shunning continued for weeks beyond the event. It started on the school bus when no one allowed me to sit with them on their seat.

"Leslie!" yelled the bus driver. "Move over and make room!" Each day he called a different person's name I was always the one who needed the seat.

When we passed out papers in class, my desk was skipped. I had to get up, walk to the teacher's desk and pick up the one extra paper.

When I approached my regular lunch table, the group stopped their conversation, refusing to look at me; if I dared to sit, a dramatic group exit followed.

I couldn't get anyone to talk with me long enough to explain what it was I did that was so wrong. I heard through tidbits from friends of friends, people whom I didn't even know. Thirty years later such "mean girl" behavior still doesn't make sense to me.

During those weeks, I drove four separate times to the local shopping center.

"Mom, I'm going up to Baskin–Robbins for some ice cream," I announced on my way out the door. And I would. I enjoyed a double scoop of mint chocolate chip on a sugar cone at the store in the very center of all the stores. But each trip, I also walked around the corner into Drug Fair, down the escalator and purchased one bottle of sleeping pills; a total of four bottles.

The first cashier—an older woman—looked at me quizzically. I smiled and said, "Oh, these are for my mom." This was the decade that treated depression with Valium. The question didn't leave her face, but she closed the sale and I walked out just as nonchalantly as I had walked in. Each visit thereafter I chose a different check out clerk, purchasing at least one other item along with a bottle of pills.

I chose a rare night when Mom and Dad were out of town and left me in the care of a neighborhood college student home on Spring Break. My parents rarely traveled together to avoid leaving the three daughters. At age 16, I was the only child remaining (my two older sisters were in college by this time).

8 pm: my plan was to swallow all four bottles, knowing no one would check in on me until six o'clock the next morning. The pills would have time to work. I planned to hide the empty bottles in separate areas so it would take that much longer for anyone to find the source of my unconsciousness; one in my clothes hamper, another on my closet shelf between my sweaters; the third under my bed in the far corner; the last on my bookshelf behind some books.

These dark thoughts contrasted with my surroundings. After my sister Gayle graduated from college, I moved into her bedroom. It was 14x15, significantly larger than my 8x9. It also had two windows allowing more sunshine. My new room was painted sunshine yellow with curtains and a bedspread patch-worked with more yellow and lime, Kelly green, and spring grass greens. I purposely chose these colors thinking if I changed my environment, I could change my perspective. Maybe the bright colors of spring would push my depression out of me as the sun coaxes the daffodils out of the ground.

Most teenage suicide attempts are cries for help; the teens survive, succeeding in bringing them the wanted attention. Mine was not a cry for help. I wanted to end my life and my misery.

Since the age of 10, I had wanted to die. Depression was never a topic of discussion in the news or in the home. I just knew I felt sad, very sad, with no source or cause, no revelation, and certainly no cure. The blackness came from somewhere deep down inside—from that big black hole inside of me that gulped down any rays of light or hope that might try to grow within.

I kept this blackness to myself as well, encapsulating it with silence. I thought if I ignored it or didn't talk about it, the depression might fade away, maybe even disappear. I was wrong. The less I talked of my depression, the more it grew, almost exponentially, especially when I felt isolated and alone. My sixteenth birthday party accelerated the depression, controlling my thoughts, words, and deeds. My depression helped me plan my death and it kept my plans silent.

I never expected the doorbell to ring that evening. It was not included in this important night's schedule with the four bottles. When I opened the door, there stood Robert, the minister from the youth group I had been attending for the past few months. The church's youth group was a new experience for me, introduced to it by a short-term boyfriend.

I had known Robert only casually for just a few months; I had not spent any one-on-one time with him, nor confided any of my pain to him. But he was always kind to me, occasionally offering a secret wink and smile. I was shocked to see him.

"Robert! Hi! What are you doing here?" I asked.

Anne, the college student staying with me, had come downstairs to see who was at the door. When I told her Robert was my youth minister, she smiled and walked back up to the master bedroom to watch television.

"I don't know," he replied, emphasizing each word rather than the casual "I don't know." His dark brown eyes peeked from his shaggy black hair that kept falling in his face. His face filled with worry. The crease deepened between his eyebrows, the corners of his mouth were turned downward with his jaw clenched and lips pursed a bit. He glanced from side to side, unsure of where to look or what to say, shaking his head in disbelief. Was there someone else with him, helping fill in the blanks of the conversation? His grimace twisted its way through the overgrown mustache, dotted with premature gray. His hands hung inside the front pockets of his well-worn jeans with just his thumbs exposed; the sleeves of his flannel shirt rolled up just below the elbows.

"What do you mean you 'don't know'?"

"I don't know why. I just had this feeling that I had to come here, right now. It couldn't wait." He kept shaking his head slightly, incredulous and very uneasy. His right hand ran through his hair while the other stayed inside his pocket. He took a slow, deep breath in and then exhaled almost as slowly.

"I have no idea why I am here; I just know I had to come over here immediately." His head turned towards me, his eyes serious, frightened, questioning. He was looking to me for the answer.

I had told no one of my intent. I had not written about my plan in my diary; I didn't have a diary. I had worked hard at not letting my discussion with family or friends raise concern. My intent was to succeed in killing myself. I had hidden this plan from everyone successfully.

This exchange between Robert and me remains a slow motion video I can replay at anytime, even now, with no deterioration of the pictures. The latter part of the conversation, after Robert came in and sat on the recovered navy blue 1950s sofa while I sat in Dad's wingback chair, is fuzzy. We talked. But I have no memory of the conversation's details. I only know that at the end of the discussion, I walked upstairs, took the four bottles out of my nightstand drawer, and brought them back downstairs to Robert. He took them with him. He appeared calm throughout the conversation, and his face brightened into relief when he took the pills into his possession, but I remember few other outward details.

What I do recall was that when Robert left that evening I felt just as sad and lonely as I had the day before. But somehow I had been able to share my plan and my pain with Robert. Something he said convinced me not to quit yet, though I have no idea today what that was. I didn't feel hopeful or relieved. I didn't feel any more "loved."

But in that moment I did feel a willingness to trust in God for one more day. I was so shocked by Robert's sudden appearance I knew it could only be God's work. Nothing else came through to me except that God wanted me around a little longer.

Before that conversation with Robert, in an adolescent immaturity, I believed my life had no impact on those around me and therefore, my death would be the same.

I felt that my existence had caused more inconvenience than joy. My parents did not speak or demonstrate this message. My perspective was just so terribly skewed and inaccurate. My perspective did not match my reality. I knew I was loved, but somehow I did not feel loved. In fact, I felt *unlovable*.

I must have been the child who needed the extra encouragement; you know, the one whom you have to say "Great job!" a thousand times before they believe you really meant it. It's not the person giving the praise who is at fault. Rather, it is the recipient who isn't hearing what is being said. I'm not certain on this; I never discussed it with anyone. I think I just heard a lot of silence. I didn't hear the 999 times before.

That night with the four bottles of sleeping pills . . . Robert's insistence on being at my home without having a clue as to why . . . Robert's conversation with me . . . this was a loud and clear message to me from God that He had a plan. I needed to trust it. God was with me even when I felt no one else was. He had proven it by sending a trusted messenger: Robert.

Betrayal

Pearls: the only precious stone made by pain, suffering, and finally, death.—Wm. Paul Young, *The Shack*

What I didn't know that evening when Robert took those four bottles of sleeping pills from me was that less than a year later, he would sexually molest me. A sexual predator had saved my life. Of course, that's not how I perceived it when it happened. But that's what happened. After that realization, I spent years questioning why God would send such a messenger. Why did God bring such a monster into my life at such a desperate moment?

At 16, I was naïve; my only experience with boys was awkward kisses and the occasional hand grabbing at my breasts to feel the flesh that barely filled a 32A bra cup. Third base was still just an analogy.

As Robert presented it to me months later, I owed 'it' to him for saving my life. He presented several other 'reasons,' as well, but the IOU was foremost in my thoughts. We never again spoke of that evening, nor what he did with the four bottles. But it was the first of many secrets between us. I was terrified Robert would someday "tell" someone of my intent to commit suicide. He knew my fear. He preyed on that fear and on my naiveté.

Building upon my fear of 'exposure,' Robert spent eight calculated months solidifying my trust, refining his pedophiliac talents to get me where he wanted me. He asked me to come early to set up for youth group. He gave me books to read that we later discussed (Annie Dillard's Pulitzer Prize winning *Pilgrim at Tinker Creek* was his current favorite); he played his acoustic guitar for me, singing songs from the Doobie Brothers; he spent hours talking to me; I wondered if this was what friendships were like; were these things friends talked about? He gave me his gray fedora hat to wear when we went on field trips. The gray in his fedora matched the premature gray in his moustache.

It started with the secret smiles and winks. It continued with raspberry picking outings. He dropped me off at home last among the youth group carpool. It even progressed in front of his wife when they invited me to their house for dinner; long, loving looks as she poured lentil soup into bowls and brought them to the table. It was our secret from everyone. I felt lucky to be chosen; to be loved, to be admired, to be someone's very special friend. Robert became a trusted, guiding spiritual figure.

During one of my early arrivals for youth group, we were in the kitchen, making baloney sandwiches that we later took to the homeless people in downtown DC. Forty slices of Wonder bread spread out on the counter, two rows of twenty. I placed two pieces of baloney on each slice of the top row. No mayonnaise or mustard; it would go bad. Bottom piece of bread on top of the baloney, into sandwich bags, then into the Igloo coolers for the car.

I hopped onto the kitchen countertop on the other side of the sink while Robert wiped up the crumbs with a damp cloth. Moving to the sink, he rinsed it out and draped it over the faucet to dry. As casually as he had moved from the other countertop to the sink, Robert moved in front of me sitting on the countertop, looked into my eyes, smiled, and slipped his hands between my knees, sliding them up my thighs, opening my legs to his approaching body. His hand brushed quickly over my pelvis, igniting it with an energy I found disconcerting, exciting, and confusing. His hands traced my hips, my waist, my breasts, and finished cupping my face. The fingers of his right hand traced through my hair, finishing at the back of my head. With this grip, Robert brought my face to his. He leaned forward and kissed me on the lips, bringing my lips open to his, thrusting his tongue in my mouth and kissing me deeply for what felt a very long time. In God's house. And then he was done. He pulled away from me, still smiling, still looking passionately and intensely at me. And then, as if nothing had transpired, Robert picked up the cooler and took it out to his car.

The kisses progressed. I remember feeling his bristly, overgrown moustache on my lips. The thick hairs reddened my lips. His rough five o'clock shadow chapped my cheeks. His guitar playing calloused fingers touched me where I had never been touched before; I had never felt a man's skin against my skin. I hadn't even passed "second base" until Robert. The rawness, redness, and soreness this man's aggression imprinted on my body matched the scars he left on my soul.

After Robert's first kiss, I didn't tell anyone. Now there were too many secrets at risk of exposure. And I didn't say anything almost a year later when Robert transferred to another church to be a youth minister for yet another group of unsuspecting, unguarded children.

Do I regret not telling anyone for decades? Absolutely. Do I wish I had acted differently? Absolutely. Am I to blame for what transpired? Absolutely *not*. It is imperative here for me to make this statement not only for myself, but for every single individual who has been or is being molested by a spiritual or religious leader. I did not cause this predator's behavior. I am not responsible for his actions upon me. I was a victim of a trusted adult who preyed on young, naïve, vulnerable children. What Robert did to me was *not* my fault.

For years, I told no one. I lived in a gagged silence. And then I spent even more years in therapy reconciling this predator's abuse; initially blaming and finding fault with myself. It took a talented therapist who explained the different types of abuse, including spiritual abuse, committed most often by a religious leader. The therapist walked me through each of Robert's carefully constructed steps, always leading me to exactly where he planned.

A crucial part of my therapy and the beginning of my healing: I wrote (and mailed) Robert a letter stating that his behavior towards me was criminal and irreprehensible. I detailed each step he took and defined it as predatory, premeditated, and sick. I told him never to contact me again or I would take my story to the police and to the church. He never contacted me again.

If you have been molested by a religious or spiritual leader, it was *not your fault*. I want you to see these words, hear them in your head, and feel them in your heart. Don't let the son of a bitch torment you for any longer than when he was lying on top of you. You deserve more. I deserved more. And I could only get more once I reconciled this abuse.

Starting to Spiral

*It's not the load that breaks you down, it's
the way you carry it.*—Lena Horne

Robert had left for another church in another state. I still
had no close friends. I worked on the high school newspaper,
sang in the concert choir. After a few months, eventually, I had
a boyfriend.

I was essentially an only child at home with my two sisters graduated from college and working in successful jobs. I
did have some periods of typical teenage happiness, giddiness,
and silliness. I could "fake it" and act "as if" for those times.
But they were short term and non-dramatic. Remember, I said
this book is not a memoir or autobiography.

My four walls of silence were strong as steel. I was silent,
but I was still miserable, hopeless. But I didn't know where to
direct the internal swirling of fear and frustration.

And then, I was introduced to wine. I did not get drunk
during the initial introduction. But the first time I got drunk,
I also experienced my first of many blackouts.

I was at a party with a bottle of Andre pink champagne.
Within two hours, I locked myself in the bathroom, vomiting
pink pizza in and around the toilet. I don't remember the rest

of the evening. I don't remember leaving the bathroom or the party. I don't remember getting home. That's pretty much how most of my drinking episodes occurred: having no memory of what happened.

Every time I drank, I experienced blackouts. I became extremely ill after each drinking episode due to a recurrence of my stomach ulcer, so I quickly became a binge drinker, imbibing only once or twice a month.

I was drunk within my first week at college. Within the first month, I had offended the girl across the hall.

"You really don't remember what you said to Serena last night?" a suitemate asked. I shook my head no, a sense of dread approaching. Alcohol had blanked my memory again; not a single brain cell revealed my actions from the night before.

Serena was very well endowed, often wearing tightly fitting white t-shirts. On the previous night, she came into my room (the party room) wearing one that read "Treasure Chest."

"WOW, I wonder what kind of treasure the guys will find in YOUR chest!" The other girls from the dorm looked at me with disgust.

My apology was met with silence; not accepted. The possibility of other friendships was broken that night. Memories of my high school shunning flooded back; depression, loneliness and hopelessness returned with the looks directed my way each time I approached the meal table.

I learned two important lessons that Sunday morning: don't drink often, and when I do, drink alone. With blackouts, getting sick every time I drank, etc., it never occurred to me to stop drinking or even decrease my intake. Rather, I chose how and where I drank; true indications of an alcoholic. Ten years later I was shocked to learn most people don't black out or get sick when they drink.

Swinging Pendulum

What gold can we mine from our darkness?—Natalie Goldberg

In high school, I worked hard to keep up appearances. I thought if I worked hard enough, people would notice and then they would like me. School did not come easily for me. I liked academic work, but it was a daily challenge for me. I graduated with a 3.3 GPA that included nightly homework, weekend studying and any extra credit projects available. It still did not come easily for me.

My parents always put education first in our lives. The three daughters never had a choice of going to college; it was mandatory. Mom and Dad felt so strongly that they paid for our Master's degrees, which each of us earned: one in psychiatric nursing, one an MBA, and mine, a Master's in Education. Dad wasn't the first one to say it, but he was the first one I heard it from: Knowledge is power. And for this child who felt powerless in many ways, knowledge gave me power and energy to take the next steps forward.

I maintained that hunger for school throughout the years. Education is a world with no boundaries (similar to my beloved southwestern desert landscape) except those of my own making and I tried very hard not to create any. I seriously contemplated going for a Ph.D. for a year or so, but marrying and having a family put that musing onto my bucket list.

The only easy task I found was writing. I loved writing. Writing was limitless in its offerings; I had no boundaries in writing. Writing gave me control and sometimes, it gave me power; I chose what I wrote, who could read and/or critique my creation, when I started and when I finished. Being co-editor of my high school newspaper and art & literary magazine, taught me skillful writing. I developed my talent and accepted others' interest and appreciation of my creations. Writing became my conduit for making noise in my silent world.

In college, I still enjoyed the academics, but struggled with course work even more, finishing with a 2.99. I was editor of the college paper, a position I coveted. I also joined a sorority, trying to become a part of—but instead it left me feeling apart from. Again. I lived in a dorm, but never connected with the girls on the hall thanks to the whole treasure chest t-shirt episode. You think elephants have a long memory; try a girls' dorm at a small southern school.

Unfortunately, going away to college did not separate me from the secrets, pain, or despair I had felt growing up. And college life did not break the binding silence.

February of my freshman year, I went to see the college psychologist. Depression had returned and I needed help.

"So what brings you here today?" he asked from behind his oak desk. It was the only question he asked. I started describing my symptoms; he quickly interrupted.

"Depression is when you are trying to find ways to kill yourself. You don't have depression. Come back to me when and if your symptoms become serious. Then I can help you." He quickly glanced at his watch and then straight at the door as if to gauge how much of his valuable time I had wasted, determined not to allow any more.

No queries about past bouts of depression, about alcohol use, about feelings of hopelessness. In less than five minutes, this bowtie wearing, khaki-clad Ph.D. decided my depression wasn't serious enough for him. He had taken my pain and desperation and thrown it like a clump of nasty dirt directly into my face. I would have to find another way to deal with my sickening infestation of darkness.

The Opposite Sex

*There's a certain class of people who will do
you in and then remain completely mysti-
fied by the depth of your pain.—Sue Grafton*

The minister and two boyfriends in high school totaled my experience with the opposite sex in high school.

My freshman year of college, I met a friend's older brother. He was in the military, the "tall, dark, and handsome" mysterious type and quite interested in me. A single night with umpteen tumblers of alcohol was all this man needed to convince me he could rescue me from my gritty, dark, caged life. Military man would lead me all over the world on exotic adventures. I was a cheap date, a cheap dreamer, and an easy mark.

I dated military man throughout college long-distance. I found his silence alluring and intriguing. The more miles apart we were, the more appealing and mysterious he became.

I attended some college functions with dates, but no one really captured me like military man had. The men on campus didn't intrigue me.

There was Tucker, who displayed me like a trophy. "THIS is my date," he announced at homecoming. He didn't speak directly to me, but instead presented me like the year's latest car model, with his hand in the middle of my back ready to turn me around, available for inspection from all sides.

There was the senior I was interested in who tried to introduce me to cocaine. Luckily, a little voice in my head warned: It may look good, but it won't feel good. I had not yet tried drugs; cocaine seemed more of a graduation drug than a beginning spot. I was still binge drinking, but not adventurous enough to move beyond alcohol yet. Three months later, two courses shy of graduating, he dropped out of college, taken hostage by cocaine addiction.

There was the crush who turned out to be gay. I think Pat Benatar is the only woman he lusted for.

My final attempt at college campus romance gave me bruises when I wouldn't have sex with him. I had brought a six-pack of Heineken—his favorite—as a congratulatory gift for a great score on his Organic Chemistry test. I thought we would sit, drink, talk, and enjoy the night. Our definitions of "enjoy the night" did not match.

"You know you want it." He was 6'2" and muscular. His family has a long famous history.

At 3 am, he let me out of his room. I ran back to the dorm room and took a long hot shower. I wanted every molecule of his drunken sweat to wash down the drain. I was not physically raped; yet emotionally, I was something. My fear had silenced me. I knew how it looked: I brought the beer and the cute figure. What was he supposed to think? With his family name, favor would never come to my side.

The next day, I watched him saunter from the frat house to the meal hall, wearing a smug grin the entire time.

Two of my college classmates lost their virginity while they were passed out drunk. One girl dropped out soon thereafter. The other woke up feeling disoriented and in terrible pain, confused by her date's motion. It was 2 am in the dorm lounge; no one around. He threw up beside her when he was done.

There were many nice guys at my school, too. Unfortunately, and bewilderingly, they weren't attracted to me. Addicts attract other addicts; thus enhancing and solidifying my warped image of the world.

Hooked

Sometimes you know before you know.—Elizabeth Berg

My senior year of college, I discovered marijuana. From my initial high, it filled the blackness that originated from so deep within. Despite the paranoia, the munchies, the hangover, I found happiness in a bong. It reminded me of my very first glass of chardonnay wine, only without the vomiting and blackout. I was hooked from the first high.

I still remember my first drink of wine: the scent rising, wafting across my face. I remember the first soft, gentle, cool sip touching my tongue, slowly sliding down my throat like liquid silk. I remember finishing the glass and wishing I could have more; much more.

My first high was not soft or gentle. The unfiltered smoke nettled my nose hairs and singed my throat as I inhaled. I coughed like a Tuberculosis patient. But by the time I finished the hit, I was wishing I could have more; much more. The addiction pendulum of drama and trauma had started swinging.

Spring of my senior year, I was student teaching. I was pressuring military man towards marriage. I had a full load of classes and working 20 hours a week in one of the campus offices.

One particular Tuesday, I was leaving to tell my parents that I was engaged to military man. My adrenal and cortisol levels had peaked, anticipating the forthcoming drama. My ulcer had converted to Irritable Bowel Syndrome with constant bouts of diarrhea, especially under stress. This day was nothing short of dehydrating.

My master teacher, having listened to my struggles between true love and unhappy parents, quietly offered me my first Valium so I could drive to the therapy session and not 'lose it,' physically or emotionally.

I took the pill, drove the three hours without interruption, remained calm and unaffected by my parents' tears in response to the ring on my left hand. I drove home and was sound asleep by 11 pm.

I didn't have to inhale, cough, soothe a scratchy throat or drop Visine into my red eyes. I didn't have to worry about throwing up, stumbling, falling down, slurring my speech, or searching for a cure for the munchies. I didn't have to do any of that.

I was addicted from my first blue pill. I even loved the V in the middle of it, which reminded me of a heart. Yes, I loved this pill called Valium and it loved me.

Starter Marriage

You develop courage by surviving difficult times and challenging adversity.—*Barbara De Angelis*

Some people may look at a specific time in their life and wish they could just erase and move on from there. Some people feel that way about my first marriage. While I don't enjoy recalling the major focal points of that relationship, my first marriage does show how some 'grains of sand' came to me and the ways I chose to deal with them. It does show important elements of how I got here from there.

I married military man in the summer of 1985, after graduating college, just months after I announced our engagement. Our honeymoon was three days in Fayetteville, North Carolina, where he was training to become a Special Forces medic. When he came home from the 16 hour day, he stepped inside, stripped down naked, leaving his clothes just inside the door, then showered, unsuccessfully scrubbing to rid his body of his patients' stench: goats. I don't remember why they used goats. I think I blocked out the reason as much as I tried to suppress the stench that activated my gag reflex and permeated every fiber of material in the room.

For three days, we ate dinner, drank, had sex, fell asleep. Our honeymoon.

Yes, I was well on my way to those exotic adventures.

Douglas Coupland first coined the phrase "Starter Marriage" in his 1991 book *Generation X*. Used as a play on the phrase "starter home," starter marriage appeared merely as a footnote in Coupland's novel. He defined it as a marriage that lasts less than five years and produces no children. I qualified. My marriage lasted just three years. Before Coupland, no one had ever written about these first-time short-term marriages much less tried to study or explain them.

The term was not in our familiar vocabulary until Pamela Paul wrote *The Starter Marriage* in 2002. Her first marriage at age 27 lasted less than a year. Paul described being "mesmerized by the romantic idea of marriage and blinded to the reality."

Yes, mine was, by definition, a starter marriage. It was also an alcoholic, abusive marriage.

Twenty plus years after my divorce, I still find the memories frightening and unnerving to recall.

The Airport: Part I

*The question is, will we use the jarring events of our
lives as excuses or opportunities?—Anne M. Johnson*

I spent our first year of marriage alone in central Virginia,
teaching. Military man transferred to the state of Washington
and then went on to Okinawa, Japan where I joined him in
May, 1986.

My parents took me to National Airport for my 24+-hour
flight from Washington, DC to Manila, Philippines where I
was to meet him while on one of his temporary duty missions.
I had never traveled internationally, much less done it alone.

My parents strongly opposed the marriage; today I can say,
rightfully so. At that time, any time that my parents and I were
together, it was tense, awkward; uncomfortable at a minimum.
I fought hard to marry military man. And now I was following
him half way around the world.

I was excited about my trip, looking forward to my exotic
adventure. I missed my husband. We were newlyweds who
had been together for less than a week's time in our first year.

Mom and Dad stood in front of me, stiff, unsure of what
to do, what to say. They were losing their baby in every way,

shape and form. They were sending me off to a man they dis-approved of. Passengers began boarding the plane. I needed to go.

I hugged Dad first. The hug was short.

But my mother's embrace was different. My arms melted around her. My head buried into her neck, smelling her Chanel Number 5 Perfume. I wanted to remember her smell; I knew it would be at least a year before I would recapture it. My tears soaked her shirt. The tears had not built, but rather just poured; an unstoppable flow from a collapsed dam. The final boarding call halted the overflow. I smiled at them both, trying to be the courageous, young married woman on the journey of her lifetime. I turned and headed down the jetway. I turned around only once, tears again pouring like an open faucet down my cheeks.

Break the Seal

They flank me—Depression on my left, loneliness on my right. They don't need to show their badges. I know these guys very well. Then they frisk me. They empty my pockets of any joy I had been carrying there. Depression even confiscates my identity; but he always does that.—Elizabeth Gilbert

The air in Manila was heavier than the August air in DC. I had traveled from the desert to DC at age 7 to Manila at age 22, each blanket of dirt and humidity heavier than the one before.

Arriving in Manila was eerily similar to arriving in Virginia that first time; stale humidity filled with jet engine fuel and sweat, with a bit of feces folded in. I felt again like I was on that rocking boat, desperately adjusting my balance in order to feel grounded and trying not to throw up from the stench or suffocating humidity.

Exhausted from the 24-hour trip in crowded coach class (back in the day when smoking was allowed on the plane and hundreds of people were coughing what I later discovered was a Tuberculosis cough), I followed the group of travelers to the agents who granted us access (or not). Zeal and excitement drained completely by hour nineteen over the Pacific

Ocean. I handed my passport to the man behind the yellowed plexi-glass.

He uttered something undecipherable.

"Pleasure," I replied. I smiled.

Silence.

I smiled more.

There was nothing to lose in translation because the official said nothing. He just sat there and glanced back at me.

I continued smiling, now feeling uncomfortable.

"Hmph," he growled.

He stamped my passport, shoving it back into my hand with his dirty hands and crusty nails. I smiled and thanked him, completely unaware of bribery as a common tradition. On my way out of the customs area, two armed guards smiled at me and directed me to a separate, empty hallway, away from other passengers. It was a suggestion with machine guns.

This did not feel right. Those short dark skinned men were smiling Cheshire cat grins. I decided it was more of an invitation than an order; if it wasn't, I'm sure they would let me know. I politely declined and followed the rest of the travelers down the crowded hallway, initially holding my breath, waiting for a gun to be jammed into my ribcage or strong arms lifting me off the floor and carrying me down the isolated hall to an even more isolated room. But they let me continue down the hall with the other passengers and I started breathing again.

Moments later, outside the building, people swarmed at me tugging my clothes, pulling my blond hair, talking to me in a tonal, unintelligible language; a few demanded I buy things in broken English; a few others were silent, pulling my suitcase almost out of my hands.

For a moment, I was back in Virginia on that July 1970 afternoon with the humidity so thick it clogged my throat and made me wonder when I would ever again take a clear breath. Manila's heat and humidity easily outranked Virginia's.

I looked up to see my Special Forces medic. At 6'4", he was easy to spot amid the 5-foot-nothing Philippinos. Grabbing my wrist, he pulled me close, taking my suitcase.

Looking into his eyes for the first time in a year, pressing my young body against his, I leaned my face toward his for a welcoming kiss.

Instead, he issued a series of commands. "Don't look at anyone. Don't talk to anyone. And don't stop. Just stay with me."

I felt crushed. Is this how honeymooners greeted one another?

I did as he ordered. Soon, we were in a tiny beige car that could have been in an American junkyard, stripped for parts. We drove from Manila to our hotel two hours away. I quickly learned some elements of this third-world nation: poverty, desperation, and filth.

With the car windows down, the pungent odor of urine wafted through the vehicle. The streets were dirt roads; no separation for cars going in opposite directions. Intersections were individual games of "Chicken" to see who would get through first without major injury. Metal scraping was acceptable. By the time we arrived at our hotel, I was vomiting outside the car. The heat and humidity, the exhaustion of a 24-hour trip, and the smells had finished me off.

The next morning, in the shower, I was washing my hair when I glanced up at the ceiling. Looking down at me was a flying cockroach at least four inches in length. I ran out of the shower screaming. Military man, trying not to laugh too hard at my hysterics, shooed the roach out of the bathroom. I rinsed quickly. Then, as I dried myself off, a small lizard ran across my bathroom floor. It was a gecko, something that most people had not heard of yet. The Geico television commercials arrived twenty years later. I was literally and figuratively worlds apart from my previous life.

Military man went to work, leaving me to tour the village alone. What better to do in a foreign country than to shop at the roadside stands, taste the food, buy some trinkets, and get acquainted with a new culture? I got acquainted all right.

Less than 500 feet from my hotel, within minutes, I found myself being pushed towards an isolated side street by a dozen or more children; yelling, making a commotion, begging for money, but this band of thieves was also working together to get me away from the crowded street. Kicking my shins, punching my ribs, grabbing my wrists, they did anything to get whatever they could from me. I realized these innocent children were pint-sized muggers who intended to inflict harm if I didn't change the direction we were taking. With no one to help me, I pushed back, kicked back, and ran back to the crowded street with two children still attached to me, determined to take anything from me they could. Moments into this new relationship, I learned a stronger way to carry myself; and the valuables I carried with me.

"We're not in Kansas anymore, Dorothy," I muttered to myself—certainly not. My first taste of being a tourist in a foreign land was nothing I had conceived of, but was something I would hold fresh in my mind for the next twenty years every time I ventured to a land whose tongue I didn't speak.

Another valuable lesson I learned after my first day in The Philippines was to make sure every drink I ordered had the bottle seal broken in my presence. Unfortunately, I didn't learn that lesson soon enough. Montezuma can exact his revenge anywhere, not just in Mexico.

When I arrived in The Philippines, I mistakenly thought I was leaving a life of doldrums and loneliness, embarking on an exciting journey with my newlywed military man and all that he promised me. Interestingly enough, as I write this, I realize he never promised me anything. He only agreed to marry me in order to keep the relationship going. Oh boy. Those two sentences should have set off a city of alarm bells for me. Unfortunately, I was so deep into my own fears and my own compulsion to "escape," I didn't see what I was actually doing.

I married an alcoholic man who refused to have a relationship based on anything more than sex and convenience. I was a traveling partner who would find him the next day after he had been drinking with the guys. He brought me to places where I could not understand the language, could not read the traffic signs, and understood nothing about the culture. Military man had brilliantly isolated me from anything, anyone and any help. The only connection I had was to him. And connecting in an emotional manner was definitely not one of his attributes.

Almost twenty years after my first experience with a sense of invisibility and isolation, I was feeling it again. This time, I had chosen to put myself in the situation and I had no idea how to get out of it. The man whom I thought was my best friend was just a bedmate. It was going to be a long stay.

Getting Sober

*Surrendering is not giving up; it is merely
moving over to the winning side.—Barbara Boyer*

While living in Okinawa, I couldn't find a job. Competition
was tough among the military wives for very few coveted posi-
tions. I even tried substitute teaching, but was never called.
As a result, I went back to graduate school for a Masters in
Education in counseling and Personnel Services.

As part of my Masters Degree program I was required to
participate in a semester-long internship that involved counseling. I initially chose one of the Department of Defense
schools, but we couldn't reach an agreement. It was down to
the wire and there weren't many choices left for this required
practicum. At the last minute, I, the binge-drinking, Valium-
popping addict, was assigned to the island's alcohol treatment
facility.

Each week, I had lunch with the Major in charge, who also
happened to be in the same Masters program. Each week, at
lunch, she told me the story of a gunnery sergeant she had to
admit to the facility for his addiction to Valium.

"That's why I am *so* glad I take it only as prescribed," I
hurriedly assured her each week. Cathy obviously knew much

more about addiction than I. She knew how to gently but firmly 'plant the seed.'

I started in recovery sideways, originally coming to Al-Anon, trying to figure out how to get military man to stop drinking. While leaving one of those Al-Anon meetings, I met someone who invited me to a speaker meeting of Alcoholics Anonymous. I attended. At my very first meeting, I heard my story from a female Navy commander. But I continued to take my carefully prescribed Valium.

A few days later, military man and I were still arguing. He was trying to convince me to stay. I refused. Besides all the 'other' reasons we already knew of, I added on that I thought he was an alcoholic. He was definitely offended by my accusation.

"Well, if I'm an alcoholic, then *you* are addicted to Valium!" he retorted. With complete commitment in my voice, I replied, "I take the Valium so I can live with *you!*" That sentence made complete sense to me at the time. I truly didn't know that most individuals don't take drugs on a daily basis in order to stay in a relationship. This statement exemplifies the level of insanity that my addiction had brought me to. And, in true, immature, unreasonable thinking, I offered a dare.

"If you stop drinking, I'll stop taking Valium, and then we'll see who's who and who's what," I pronounced, steadfastly certain in my conviction that military man would certainly drink before I ever took another Valium.

I don't know how long it was before military man took his next drink. For me, it's unimportant. What is important is the events of the next three days for me. Up to now, I have described what it was like before. Now comes the part of what happened.

I had no concept of time during these three days. I remember only snippets, thankfully. But they are some of the most important, cataclysmic moments in my life that laid the foundation for how I have chosen to live each day since.

Even though I was an intern at the island's alcohol treatment facility, I did not enter treatment when I chose to stop taking Valium. Instead, I stayed at home and acted as if life was normal. I was working at my desk in the back bedroom when I heard voices in the living room. I walked down the hallway, following the voices. When I got to the living room, there was no one around. I glanced outside to see if maybe I heard one of our too-close neighbors in their yard. No one. I felt confused, trying to sort out exactly what I heard. Was it a man's voice? Children playing?

As I turned around, my forearms started to itch. I scratched them both in long, vertical motions. Glancing down to see what was making them itch, I suddenly saw black spiders crawling on my arms, coming out of no where at my wrists towards the bend at my elbow. Screaming, I tried to scratch them off my arms, but they kept coming.

There is a scene in the classic television series M*A*S*H where a nurse drops her meal tray in the mess tent and starts scratching at her arms furiously, screaming, "Make them stop! Make them stop! Help me! I can't get them off of me!" It turns out she was in the beginning stages of the DTs, from her withdrawal from alcohol.

In the same moment that I tried to scratch the spiders off my own arms, I remembered this scene from M*A*S*H and realized that I was beginning my own withdrawal from Valium. The voices I had heard minutes before were auditory hallucinations. It was this moment, in the middle of my living room, that I realized and accepted I was indeed addicted to Valium.

I am not proud of this moment. It is not one I share with others often, and rarely have I done so outside of a 12-Step Recovery program meeting. It was hard to live through then.

And it is difficult to walk through now, 22+ years later. But this is the moment that lay to rest every doubt about whether or not I had a "problem" with Valium. The next few days remain fuzzy for me. I was in and out of lucidity, wracked with insomnia, sweating, blurred vision, tingling, diarrhea, haunted by more hallucinations. I know now that going through Valium withdrawal without medical supervision is not only dangerous, but can actually be fatal. I didn't know that then. But I also didn't think I had a problem. For whatever reason, I survived the withdrawal, and some of it remains a mystery to me, but I remember enough to know to my core that I am an addict.

I believe that time period was a gift of God's grace. I have no other way to explain why I did not die or suffer permanently disabling seizures. And I don't really need to explain anything about those days. I know, at one point, I wanted to die. I wanted the pain to stop. And I know God was with me. I know He suffered with me through each terrifying, gritty symptom. In the midst of that suffering, I know I made a decision that I wanted to live more than I wanted to die. I didn't know how to live. I didn't know how I would be able to live life on life's terms. But I know God carried me to the end of that journey so I could start a new one. In those few days, God brought me to the point of willingness again, to start down a path with an unknown destination.

I decided to attend a Narcotics Anonymous meeting since my primary drug of choice was Valium, not alcohol. I attended for a week, introducing myself as, "Hi, my name is Sharon and I'm an addict."

A chorus of voices responded: "AND AN ALCOHOLIC IN DENIAL."

"What?" I shot back, offended. "I only drink like once a month. I'm *not* an alcoholic. Valium is the only drug I have a problem with." I was confused, a bit put off, and trying to figure out what everyone was laughing about.

Actually, I was really angry. I had just gone through hell getting off the Valium and now these people were asking me to stop drinking as well? Maybe this 12-Step Program wasn't for me after all. Here I am, just coming off my drug of choice, newly separated, frightened of my husband, in a foreign country with no money, and now they want me to stop drinking too? I thought they were being quite insensitive to the severity of my situation; and they were being rude about it by laughing at my response.

"I only drink once a month, and then, never more than two glasses," I tried justifying to anyone around me. "I can't drink anymore or I get sick."

It took me only a week of meetings, seven times, to get the drift. They suggested I try controlled drinking.

"Try buying a bottle, and drinking just two glasses," Cliff offered. "Then call me tomorrow and let me know how it worked out." He smiled, hugged me, and left.

Someone just gave me permission to get drunk. That was kinda cool. I bought a bottle of my favorite, Korbel Brut, and put it in the fridge. After dinner, I got out my favorite champagne glass, opened the bottle with a pop, and poured my first glass.

The scent wafted to my face, bubbles tickling my nose, misting my upper lip. Sweetness in a glass. Escape in a glass. The first glass emptied quickly. I poured the second glass and tried to sip it. But I wanted the effect more than I wanted to enjoy the taste. I wanted to get drunk and not to feel. And I wanted it in a hurry. In a matter of minutes, the glass transformed from Sweetness to Escape to Oblivion. I wanted oblivion in a glass. I had always wanted the oblivion; I just didn't want to admit.

There's a saying in AA that a thousand drinks is not enough and a single drink is too much. This alcoholic/addict never wanted *a* drink or *a* Valium. I wanted enough wine or drugs so I would stop feeling, stop thinking, stop hurting. I could not handle life on life's terms. The only way I knew to survive was to escape in any way possible. And my escape was through as many glasses of alcohol or as many pills as my body would accept until I passed out.

During the entire second glass of the Korbel Brut of this 'controlled drinking' exercise, I obsessed over how I would explain to everyone at the meeting why I needed more than two glasses of champagne.

Eventually, I teetered to the kitchen sink, pouring out less than an ounce of the remaining silk liquid, determined that I wouldn't have to admit to drinking the "whole bottle." It was September 12, 1988. I have not had a drink since. Each year, on my anniversary, I write Cathy, the treatment center major, a Thank You note for planting that seed. To date, she has received more than 20 Thank You notes.

I think my acceptance of being an alcoholic was easier to reach because of the severity of the Valium withdrawal. I don't think that my body was addicted to alcohol, but it was easier to make that mind/body connection and to see that I drank to escape, to get away, just as I had popped the Valium.

It was still difficult, though, to realize that I could no longer drink or drug as a way to "cope with life." Like the scratches on my forearms, I felt raw and exposed. I felt brittle, as though a single unkind word would shatter my bones into thousands of pieces on the floor. I was very, very fragile in a very, very tough situation. I didn't know if I would survive.

I thought that day was the end of my life. It was the end of the world as I knew and understood it. I was taking another step into the unknown, again, onto a path unknown, grappled with fear and anxiety. Those first days are where I learned the importance of doing things one at a time; one minute at a time, one hour at a day, one day at a time. Sometimes the things I was doing included just breathing, just being, just keeping my body alive.

I had taken the first step in surrendering my life as a practicing addict/alcoholic, freeing me from a life of bondage to alcohol and a blue pill with a V in the middle that looked like a little heart.

Ode to My Disease

I have a daily reprieve from a disease
that I have had since birth and will die with.

It is a disease by genetics; not willpower or choice.
Treatable, not curable.

It sprouted at age 13 with a single glass of white wine.
It raged in my early twenties, mixing wine, daiquiri, beer, and any old booze.
It quieted on September 12, 1988
with a bottle of Korbel Brut.

On that hot, humid, September eve, I began
a trek that now, beyond year twenty.
I surrendered that night, on a cliff overlooking the ocean.
Instead of jumping off the cliff to rocks below, I
Started my journey of Recovery.

The directions are clear:
Don't drink
Go to Meetings
Pray
Work the Steps

Twelve Steps structure my path. They are my map.
I won't finish these steps; I find new
ways to travel through them.

The disease whispers in my ear.
I can still take a drink if I want; I should take a drink.

But the clichés scream, silencing addiction's whispers.
One day at a time.
Progress; not perfection.
Do the next right thing; the next most loving thing.
Acceptance is the answer to all my problems.
Patience and tolerance.

My disease had to erupt in order for my soul to heal.
I had to be there then in order to be here now.
Everything in my life happened for a reason that I may
never understand or even know. But I know that my life
now is greater than I had ever dreamed of or hoped for.
And for that I will always be grateful.

**I am Sharon
And I am a
Grateful Recovering Addict and Alcoholic**

Quick Demise

*Every action we take, everything we do, is either
a victory or defeat in the struggle to become
what we want to be.—Anne Byrhhe*

Certain American military units spend most of their time training in other locations, leaving families behind for extended periods of time. In the two and a half years of my stay on the also hot and humid island of Okinawa, military man and I were together for approximately five months total.

It was a quick demise.

As usual in our arguments, I was desperately trying to get the man to 'talk' so we could resolve our issues. Outside, the waves of the Sea of Japan crashed against the beach just a few hundred yards away from the house, though usually the sound of the waves fell into a background din because of its constancy. He laid on the sofa, refusing to look at me or even acknowledge my presence, or respond to my questions. He uttered no words; his clenched jaw and crossed arms conveyed his anger. I was frustrated; a one-way monologue does not make a conversation and certainly does not lead towards compromise, negotiation, or resolution.

I was exasperated.

"I've had it. If you aren't going to talk to me, there is no sense in my sticking around here."

I stood up, grabbed the car keys and headed for the door. Military man leapt from the sofa and grabbed my arms.

"You aren't going anywhere unless I say you can go." A once-familiar marital argument had ratcheted to a new level of gut-wrenching panic, anger, despair. Filled with rushing adrenaline, I wrestled myself free, though losing the car keys in the midst. I ran out the door to the yard. Having no vehicle, and really having nowhere to go, I stood outside on that hot, humid August day, my skin clammy and my sobs unstoppable, rubbing my arms where the bruises later surfaced, facing the house in case he came out after me. Silent streams of tears fell down my cheeks. I searched for my next move.

For a moment, the wallop of the waves faded, my tears stopped, my body stopped shaking. Deep down inside of me, way down deep, in a place previously unknown; I heard it: a solid, honest, compassionate whisper. It was quiet, very quiet. But it was clear. And it was true.

"If you go back into that house, you will never come back out."

I had been protected this far, but there was no promise of protection if I walked back through that door. That was the first time I heard the voice of God, though, at the time, I did not recognize it as such.

I walked to an American neighbor's house and began the process of divorcing military man.

Airport: Part II

I wanted a perfect ending. Now I've learned, the hard way, that some poems don't rhyme, and some stories don't have a clear beginning, middle, and end. Life is about not knowing, having to change, taking the moment and making the best of it without knowing what's going to happen next.—Gilda Radner

Two and a half years later, my parents and I were at the airport again.

When the marriage started dive-bombing, I called my Aunt Betty, Dad's sister, trying to figure out how to ask for help from my parents to get off the island. By this point, military man had emptied and closed our bank account and canceled our credit card accounts. I was desperately trying to figure out how to get away while military man was exerting all pressure possible from all angles to force me to come back to him.

There is a Hell on earth; living with an abusive partner and living in the midst of alcoholism and addiction each qualify. I got the double header.

I had only one way to escape and it was with the help of my parents.

"Dad, I need help," I sputtered out in a rare overseas phone call.

He and Mom helped me. They got money and a plane ticket to me. I cried as the plane lifted from the runway and the wheels locked back into flying position. I had escaped. I was relieved, though still frightened. I was flying into an unknown life. Sometimes, fear of the unknown can make people stay in an ugly situation. But I knew the only thing worse than leaving was staying. If I stayed parts of me would die on a daily basis. If I left, I might have a chance to live again.

My thoughts blurred with exhaustion; my emotions raw. I didn't know what would happen. I knew if I wanted to live, I needed to leave military man and stay as far away from him as possible.

I got off the airplane at Dulles airport, walked down the jetway into the open area, and Mom and Dad took me into their arms with heavy sobs and utter relief.

Years later, Mom said, "You looked like something the cat dragged in. Your hair was flat and stringy; your skin pale and dull. Your face was completely empty, void of emotion; you looked like you had just survived a traumatic event and were walking around in shock."

Dad added, "You looked like a sick, abused, abandoned puppy."

Twenty years later, the tears still surface when each of us recalls that moment.

Home

One faces the future with one's past.—Pearl S. Buck

Since the move to Virginia so many years before, at age 7, I had felt disconnected, isolated, confused, and trapped. I left my El Paso home and had not yet found anything closely resembling it. In adulthood, turmoil had become my only constant. Sometimes it was cast upon me; but sometimes, I created my own. After a few years of disconcerting events and emotions, my body and brain adjusted, thinking it to be the "new normal."

I believe this physical and emotional turmoil is also an element of alcoholism. Though I had not started drinking yet, alcoholism had trained my brain in the how to attract and be attracted to unhealthy people in unhealthy situations.

My return from Okinawa to my family back in Virginia was the closest feeling I had in 15 years to a Pollyanna-ish definition of "being home." The essential elements were there: returning to a safe place welcomed by people who loved me in an atmosphere of harmony, forgiveness, and acceptance.

By the age of 25, my brain, body, and soul had diminished to a fleck. I had escaped an abusive, destructive marriage; I had surrendered my addiction to drugs and alcohol. I was starting to grasp the adage: "No matter where you go, there you are."

Geographic cures no longer worked. I had lost all my 'friends.' I had my two cats, Charley and Hodges, and my family. I was jobless, homeless, and had no money. My work had just begun. My job: healing.

Nine Months

You, alone, are enough.—Maya Angelou

It took me the same amount of time to build a foundation for sober living and healthy relationships as it takes to create and birth a child.

The first six weeks after I left Okinawa, I lived with Mom and Dad. A friend of theirs, familiar with my situation, offered me an efficiency apartment he owned just three miles into town. The two cats, Charley and Hodges, and I moved in, dotting the 500 square-feet with a navy blue sofa covered in bright orange flowers, a pink and purple flowery futon (I like flowers), a 19" black-and-white television, and a bamboo screen. A table and two chairs were already there and Mom and Dad loaned me two lamps, dishes, and glasses. It was home.

No one dictated where the furniture went, no one asked what was for dinner. My primary responsibility was feeding the cats. At this early point in my healing, it was all the responsibility I wanted. I needed this time to focus on me; to get to know the sober Sharon. I had to figure out what made me happy, what gave me focus, what was important to me.

Quickly, I developed a routine. The routine helped the healing process. It gave me structure. It eliminated any sense of surprise, which at that point, I really didn't want anymore surprises in my life. Routine gave me the foundation for creating a healthier life.

For most of the day I sat in silence on the full size sofa completing intricate counted cross-stitch projects, Charley curled on the cushion next to me; Hodges outstretched by the window, warming his fur in the afternoon sun. The largest and most detailed project was a graphic version of The Lord's Prayer. It became my daily mantra. Sometimes, I just sat and petted my cats, dreaming about being a cat with only a cat's problems. Sometimes, I watched television, but it was rare. The shows only seemed to insert noise rather than information or entertainment into my brain. For laughter, I watched "The Cosby Show," a few episodes of "Golden Girls," and a new show, "America's Funniest Home Videos." Laughter helped me to heal, but it came slowly to me. Mostly, I sat in silence. This silence helped heal me, comforting and reassuring me that all would eventually be ok. It was not vengeful or heavy. Rather, it wrapped around me like my grandmother's hand knitted afghan, keeping the draft and the cold away.

I learned silence grounds me. Instead of feeling inundated by outside voices, I had the time and space to go within, to hear what my heart was asking for, yearning for. In the quiet, I could hear the answers. Any decisions I make must be based on love; for myself, my friends, and for God.

Listening to my heart was healing for me. It gave me time to develop my own sense of self again, unencumbered by anyone else's demands. I was learning in baby steps. I stopped letting people tell me who I should be.

I broke up my days by attending local meetings of Alcoholics Anonymous. Sometimes I went to one meeting a day, often two. I listened to the stories, studied and worked the Steps, and tearfully shared my own experience. Others told their respective stories, their own contributions of strength and hope. I held onto the offerings, hoping one day, I would have my own.

"Keep coming back." I took the words literally.

"How often should I attend meetings?" I asked.

"Every day until someone tells you to stop," was the reply. I took that literally, too. But it's what I needed to heal. I attended an AA meeting every day for the first two years of my sobriety.

Sometimes, I joined the group for lunch or dinner afterwards. Slowly, I developed friendships. I went to sober parties. I went shopping with friends. I taught a few how to do needlepoint and how to knit. Yes, this is a part of my life that definitely included "happy times." As we each began our journey, we learned the importance of connecting, of laughing with one another (not at one another), of sharing our lives. We worked the 12 Steps of Alcoholics Anonymous. We opened our hearts to one another and we accepted each other, character defects and all.

When I wasn't with my sober friends, I was often with Mom and Dad. I was at their house at least three times a week. In my depression and addiction, I had brought only unhealthy people into my life. New into sobriety, I didn't want to make the same mistake. Mom and Dad were the only people I could trust myself with.

The silence, the meetings, the laughter and sharing; each of these was a critical part of creating a healthier way to live.

The Aha! Moment

Hope… is not a feeling; it is
something you do.—Katherine Paterson

When I describe to others some of the circumstances in my life, or things that happened to me, I will often hear the question, "How did you get out of it?" or "How did you get from there to where you are now?"

Initially, I used to shrug my shoulders, wondering the same thing. I am not anyone 'special' or 'gifted.' I often felt ashamed for even being in those circumstances. I should have known better or I should have realized what was happening earlier on. But I didn't, so, as it goes, no matter where I went, there I was.

The nine months I spent ensconced in my efficiency apartment afforded me the time, the space, the energy, and the quiet to be able to start listening to my heart. I could ask questions and begin to hear some answers. If the answers didn't appear, possibilities did.

For each instance, the possibilities were different. Sometimes, they were clouded in fog, weighted in darkness.

I was blind and deaf, desperately searching for something to make sense; for the world to connect back with me. Previously, feeling utterly alone at each desperate moment, I pictured myself as that young girl with arms outstretched. Only in those times, my arms were waving wildly; primal, guttural screams for help.

But things were changing. I didn't always have to wave and scream and thrash. I was beginning to learn: in order to listen to my heart, I needed to silence myself. I needed to quiet everything around me and inside of me. I needed to listen.

When I was standing outside my house in Okinawa, it had been a voice deep down inside. With my last drink, it was the final wine droplets landing in the sink.

Some call it a moment of clarity or divine intervention, or a spiritual awakening. I call it an Aha! moment. It is the moment when I can hear, when I know, that an answer is being offered to me. All other sounds measurably fade, including the banter in my brain. It is when the answer travels from my heart to my head and says, "This is so." No questions follow, no objections interrupt; just the recognition that I must listen and follow.

My *Aha!* moment is actually not a moment; instead, it is a three-step process. But the process transpires in seemingly nano-seconds. For me, each of the following three elements must occur in order for the defining moment to succeed:

A—Acceptance
H—Hope
A—Action

The Aha! moment transforms me from feeling lonely, hopeless fearful and desperate to being willing to try something new, to venture into the unknown, to take the leap.

Acceptance

I first heard about acceptance in tangible, definable terms when I stopped drinking and taking Valium in 1988 and entered the rooms of Alcoholics Anonymous. In the 3rd edition of the *Alcoholics Anonymous* book reads,

> "Acceptance is the answer to all my problems today. When I am disturbed, it is because I find some person, place, thing, or situation—some fact of my life—unacceptable to me, and I can find no serenity until I accept that person, place, thing, or situation as being exactly the way it is supposed to be at this moment" (p. 449).

A lightning bolt struck me the first time I read this paragraph. Ok, it wasn't a lightning bolt. But it was those goosebumps on my arms, a spooky music playing moment. I took a small gasp of air, thinking this must be what an archaeologist feels as he gently brushes away the sand from a great discovery.

From childhood, I thought acceptance meant I condoned or approved of things. That whatever had happened to me was ok by me; that I had essentially given permission for whatever came my way. Acceptance ranged from Kraft Macaroni and Cheese for dinner to molestation by a youth minister.

I couldn't do that. I couldn't accept the bad things. I thought by hiding the dramas and traumas, surely they would disappear from my reality, or at least from my memory.

When I read page 449 of the Big Book I realized that by accepting my reality, I was not responsible for what others had done to me. Accepting was not the same as giving permission. Accepting was not the same as liking or condoning or approving.

Acceptance was an acknowledgement.

I could accept my circumstances, my life, people, and even events around me, *without* giving my approval or releasing my control over such. I don't have to like what happened; I just need to accept that it indeed occurred.

This was a big moment for me. This meant that I could (and should) acknowledge everything that happened to me. This moment gave me permission to accept my role, whether it was as a victim, an instigator, or a bystander.

Twenty plus years later, I have to pause and take a breath here. Just by closing my eyes, I am back in that moment of truth, that moment of learning what Acceptance is and needs to be. I get the goosebumps again. I get short of breath and have to remind myself to breathe inward slowly and deeply. As I exhale, I bring myself forward again to the present.

With acceptance I learned how to apologize, how to behave proactively rather than reactively, and how to live life without as much worry. Acceptance doesn't mean that life gets better; it just means that my way of living life on life's terms improves.

Hope

The evening when I planned to consume all four bottles of sleeping pills at age sixteen was not the only time I had wanted to kill myself. There were other times when the hopelessness was overwhelming. But each time, I heard, saw, or felt a sign that said, "not yet." Something would distract me from the despair just long enough for me to decide to give life another hour, another day. That something was often a phone-call, or an unannounced visitor; sometimes it was my ability to write out my despair on a piece of paper. And sometimes, the distraction was sleep. Regardless of what it was, it created a critical moment of hope; a moment that became a willingness to choose life for just a bit longer. It was a moment; an instant, when I wanted to live just a little more than I wanted to die.

Action

Through each crisis in my life, with acceptance and hope, in a single defining moment, I finally gained the courage to do things differently. I leapt toward faith, stepping into the unknown. I developed a willingness that was previously absent, non-existent. I learned if I didn't have the willingness, I could also pray for the willingness to be willing. Sometimes, the action was getting onto a plane, leaving everything behind me; and sometimes, it was just getting up out of bed in the morning. My actions took the form of believing in the possibilities instead of focusing on where I felt stuck. The cliché "Fake it 'til you make it" fits appropriately here.

It didn't mean my depression disappeared or improved significantly. It meant as each moment or each day passed, I was able to put one foot in front of the other and do something with the hope that 'it' would get better, even in miniscule increments. I knew if I stayed where I was, nothing would get better; nothing would change. If I wanted to ease the pain, I had to try something different.

That is where my *Aha!* came from. The pain had to be great enough for me to accept my reality, to hope that something different, and hopefully better, was out there and to do whatever came next to reach that point. It seems clear and simple when I write it down on paper. But I also know just because something is simple, it does not mean it is easy.

It was simple to see bruises on my arms: it was not easy to leave an abusive relationship. It was simple to see how sick I got every time I drank wine, but it was not easy to get sober. It was simple to enter into a room full of people, but it was not easy to feel *a part of* them, rather than *apart from* them.

Love Story

You know I love you still.
Will I wait a lonely lifetime,
If you want me to, you know I will.
— Paul McCartney

At age 25, I was healing from an abusive marriage, addiction, and a humungous lack of self-esteem and self worth. After nine months of solitary life, I accepted a teaching position at a local middle school. I had no interest in dating for months. When I did start back into the dating realm, it was often a man who wanted a pitcher of beer at dinner, sex after dinner on the first date, or both. I felt fragile and didn't know how to get through this horrendous process. It ended up being simpler to date sober guys.

I met Jeffrey in a church parking lot. I was with a current boyfriend; we were all going to the same meeting (Jeff has given me permission to break his anonymity). That boyfriend and I eventually broke up but Jeff and I kept attending the same meeting: Saturday evening 11th Step AA meeting. That is where we fell in love.

Jeff fell in love with how my hands move as I knitted for the hour. I fell in love with Jeff's devotion to God, his faith, his rootedness in family. Each weekly meeting focused on maintaining a conscious contact with God on a daily basis. In some respects, it was easy to fall in love in this meeting because each week was a spiritual experience, filled with hope as people shared their own experiences of living life while staying connected to a power greater than themselves.

It still took another six months, another boyfriend for me, and another girlfriend for Jeff before we figured out we should be dating one another and not anyone else. So that's what we did.

This is where a starter marriage can come in handy. We both knew what we wanted, didn't want, what was acceptable, and what the deal breakers were. It was a shorter interview process.

On an April afternoon, I came in from shopping with my mom, turned on the machine and heard this slightly higher than usual pitched voice:

> Uh, hello Sharon. It was really great to see you yesterday at the meeting. I'm sorry we didn't have much opportunity to talk and catch up with one another. So, umm . . . I was wondering if you would like to go out on a date with me. I was thinking Chinese, but whatever you prefer is fine. If you are interested, please give me a call...."

Our first date was at a local Chinese restaurant. He drove his baby blue Dodge Dakota with the passenger side filled with papers, coffee cups, a measuring tape, pencils, and a small block of wood.

"I'm sorry. My truck isn't usually this messy," he mumbled as he threw the mess behind the two seats of the cab. The crispy shrimp with walnuts wasn't great, but we spent an hour and a half talking and laughing. I saw a sparkle in his slate blue eyes that evening that I had not seen in any other man I had dated. Jeff has cute, baby pink lips that almost hide between his neatly trimmed moustache and beard; he doesn't let the hair grow over them. We kissed for the first time two dates later, after another dinner. Then we kissed again after a walk in the county parkland, hypnotized by the blooming daffodils, crocuses, and Virginia bluebells.

Mostly, I was mesmerized by Jeff's intensity and calmness. He also had the sexiest strongest forearms from swinging a hammer at work all day. I loved to run my fingers along his arms, up to his biceps. I loved feeling those arms wrap around me, shielding me, protecting me. Jeff was tall, dark, handsome, and *not* mysterious, *not* silent. He talked with me for hours, inviting me into every part of his life, his story, his soul. He wanted me to know everything about him. We did not want mystery in our second marriages. We aimed for full disclosure, faults and all.

I met Jeff's two children, Heather and Joey, and also his sister and father on the next date. Jeff doesn't like to draw things out.

"I just figured it was sink or swim if my family didn't like you," he later stated. "I didn't want to waste my time dating someone my family didn't like." Luckily, I passed the family test.

Four months later Jeffrey told me he loved me for the first time as we swam in a private pool. The summer sun had warmed the water; it was an unusual August day with low humidity. The Virginia air was actually pleasant to breathe in. There was nothing to the day's agenda except swimming, sun-bathing and salmon on the grill for dinner. It was a perfect day to hear, "I love you," to kiss in the water, to hold hands, to drink iced tea as the sun dried our bathing suits.

Jeff asked me to marry him on the playground, next to the merry-go-round, an hour before I had Back-to-School night with my students' parents. I don't remember much of the evening's program, but I remember that moment on the playground. I remember I was wearing a blue dress with small floral print. In fact, I recall it was the same blue dress I wore on our first date; and the same blue dress I wore when I told Jeffrey we were having a baby. I should have kept that dress.

We married during my school's Spring Break eleven and a half months after we started dating. The night before our wedding, I stayed up late worrying more about becoming a step-mother than becoming Jeff's wife. I was unsure how I would be able to handle part-time weekend parenting—more on that later. But I was certain I wanted to marry this man and stay with him forever. I had never been so certain about another person in my entire life.

Nineteen years later, Jeff still has slate blue eyes that spar-kle, we still go out to dinner and talk and laugh. He hugs me in the middle of the night during a thunderstorm. He tickles me. He wants me. He defends me to anyone who criticizes me. He is also honest with me and calls me on my bluffs. He does not pretend. He created a large organic garden during my recent battle with advanced Lyme disease. He is indeed, my rock solid foundation, with good compost soil!

A few years after Jeff and I married, a month shy of my 30th birthday, I gave birth to our son, Stephen. The last ten weeks of pregnancy were complicated, spent on bed rest and Turbutaline, otherwise known as the 'drug from hell' as it causes shakiness, lack of concentration, irritability, headaches, increased sweating, and heart palpitations. A healthy pregnant woman can be difficult to deal with, but a woman carrying a high-risk pregnancy and ingesting Turbutaline is just not pleasant.

I held onto the pregnancy until 39 weeks. My water broke at 3 am. I never had little contractions. There was no progressing labor for me. Instead, my contractions started at 3 minutes apart at 4:10 am. I did the classic movie scene where the wife cusses out the husband and calls him every name in the book. There sat Jeffrey, trying to help me focus on my breathing and I'm yelling at him to get out of my face.

"You're not doing it right," I screamed at him. "If you can't breathe right, then get the hell out of my face!" His face looked bewildered and betrayed. And I didn't care. I just needed someone who would breathe right. In the intensity, Jeff came forward again, holding me, encouraging me as I started pushing. Three pushes, then I fainted. Yes, you can faint even when lying down. It's called a Vasovegal Response. Smelling salts brought me back, but when I fainted, Stephen's heartbeat stopped.

The medical team tried shaking and pushing my belly, trying to revive the baby inside. Doctors and nurses alike shouted orders, reported vitals. They rolled me onto my hands and knees, shaking and pushing my belly again, hoping for a positive response. Every second counted.

The pain was immeasurable for me. Through my exhaustion and confusion, the obstetrician lowered her face within inches of mine and said in a very calm, matter of fact, authoritative tone, "We have lost the baby's heartbeat and nothing is working to get it restarted. We have to get your baby out NOW." I nodded in agreement, not really knowing what she meant.

"We don't want him pushing any farther down the canal; there's no time. So we're going to take you down the hallway to surgery and we're going to do a C-section. We're going to get this baby out as fast as we can, ok?" I nodded again, understanding more, but unable to utter any words.

As they rolled me out, my last look at the room framed Jeffrey standing there, alone. I *knew* I would be all right. I hoped and expected the baby would be all right. We both had a lot of medical staff working on us. But I didn't think Jeff would be all right. I knew he shouldn't be alone.

"Call Mom and Dad!" I shouted. "Get them down here to stay with you." He nodded, fright-filled tears running down his face, wondering if this would be the last time he would see his wife alive.

Because my labor progressed so quickly, I never got an epidural, so the emergency C-section required general anesthesia. I woke up 45 minutes later, cussing like a sailor and asking to see my baby. Jeffrey stood beside me, leaned down next to my ear and said, "It's ok, sweetie. The baby is going to be fine. You're ok. You can see him soon; they're just running some tests on him." I drifted in and out of morphine consciousness, each time, using the F-word a little more and wanting my baby even more.

Each time I woke, Jeff was there beside my gurney, holding my hand or stroking my hair.

"Do you want to see your parents?" he asked. "They're here. They want to come in here and see you."

"Not until I can stop saying F---; where's the baby? Where is he? Is he ok?"

A slight pause later, Jeff bent down again and with more tears falling, he said, "There's something wrong with him, Sharon, but it can be fixed. He has to have surgery, but he's going to be ok." I faded back into morphine oblivion.

Stephen was born with a birth defect that happens in about 1 out of every 4000 children: tracheal esophageal fistula. The corrective surgery for this defect had only been created twelve years prior. The local hospital surgeon did about one of these repairs a year; the surgeon at Children's Hospital in Washington, DC., performed about one a month. Jeff figured the odds for success and made the decision easily. To Children's Hospital Stephen went.

Stephen went into surgery when he was 12 hours old and came out four hours later, the recipient of a successful, but complicated repair. He was not out of the woods yet.

The next morning, Jeff entered my hospital room. The first words we both uttered were: "We need to get him baptized." Yes, this man, my husband, was my foundation in a world that had just turned us upside down and inside out.

Jeff arranged for our minister to come to my hospital room. With Jeff, my dad and sister Gayle present, he blessed the bottle of water we had and held the first part of the baptism at the foot of my bed, our hands clasped tightly in one another's. Then, the four of them trekked to Children's Hospital, where Stephen was baptized, surrounded in love, prayer, and faith by family and nursing staff.

In turbulent times, Jeff does not fade away. He stands firm. He is a man of action; he usually tries to *do* something that will help the current crisis. His faith is deep and profound. He shares it freely with me in all elements of our marriage; from courting me as every woman dreams of, to taking care of our newborn, sick son when I could not. And sometimes, he shares his love and honor in other ways.

Early in our marriage, I arrived home from a long day of teaching English to 140 8th graders. My mantra was the same on the tough days, "Don't touch me and don't talk to me for the next 30 minutes." I needed a period of time when someone wasn't calling, "Mrs. Rainey, Mrs. Rainey, I need your help." I needed time when someone wasn't pulling at my sleeve or waving their hand in front of my face, or shoving a late homework paper on top of my grade book.

It was one of those days when Jeff greeted me at the door with a sweet, silent smile. He took my briefcase and my purse from my hands and laid them on top of the desk. Still silent, he motioned for me to come upstairs, to follow him. As we reached the top floor, he arrived at the bathroom door and stood to the side, motioning me to enter. I looked in, still trying to decipher his plan and still exhausted from my day; a dozen candles gently lit the room, a hot bubble bath waited for me. He smiled.

"Take as long as you want. Enjoy the silence." And he left. I slipped into the bubbles and relished in the extravagance. A half hour later, he tapped on the door, silently entered, and handed me a cup of homemade hot cocoa with whipped cream he had also made from scratch. He kissed me on the forehead and left me again to soak in the solitude.

· · ·

During one of our trips to Taos, New Mexico, Jeff went fly-fishing with a local guide. They talked a bit as they traversed over rocks and through brush to get to the 'right' spot on the Red River. One of the guide's questions included, "What does your wife do?"

Without missing a beat, Jeff replied, "She's a writer."

"Oh! What does she write?" he asked.

"She writes essays about her life, our family, things going on and how they affect her, how her perception of the world and of humanity change and yet really don't change. She writes a lot about her relationship with God." Jeff offered back.

This was a profound moment for me and I wasn't even there. I only heard about it later when Jeff and the guide returned to the hotel. The guide's parting words to me were, "Good luck on your writing! I would love to read your book when it comes out!"

I turned around to Jeff, stunned. He told me how the discussion started and what he had said. Crybaby me started the tears.

"Did I do something wrong?" Jeff asked. I was trying to catch my breath before I could release the words: "No one has ever called me a writer before." He smiled, tilted his head a little to the right, and replied, "Well, you are a writer, so you better get used to it." And then he kissed me gently on the lips.

Jeff thinks I'm a writer. And that's what he tells other people! I guess if he's saying it, maybe I better start acting like one. As we got the rest of the gear packed into the car, I felt a resurgence of my self-esteem, pride. The drive out of Taos back down to Santa Fe gave me time to write even more so; this time, with a little more inspiration and energy.

Hyper-Sensitive, Over-Reactive, Over-Protective

Being a parent means you go through life with the invisible muzzle of a gun held to your head. You may have the greatest joy you ever dreamed of, but you will never again draw an untroubled breath.—Anne Lamott

Though the surgical repair for Stephen's birth defect (aka TEF) was considered successful, it came with complications. One of those was a weak trachea, which led to recurrent lung infections. The first few years of his life were spent in six-week cycles: a week getting sick, a week going to the pediatrician three times to ask for antibiotics, ten days on antibiotics and then two weeks getting well. And then it started all over again.

During those first five years, I signed up with five different pediatric groups, hoping each time for a smarter, more current physician who would understand a special needs child. By this time, I knew Stephen needed Zithromycin to heal the pneumonia and it usually took two dosings, not just one. I didn't like to play the "doctor knows best" game either. So I usually went in telling the physician what was wrong and what we needed.

One particular week, I went to the practice three times: Monday, Wednesday, and Friday. Each time, I told them it was pneumonia and that we needed to get Stephen started on Zithro as quickly as possible. Each time, I got the hand pat, the patronization that "I'm the physician, you are not; I know what's best for your child." After the Friday appointment, still with no antibiotic, I drove directly to the emergency room and had Stephen's chest x-rayed. He had double pneumonia.

The following Monday, I returned to the same pediatrician, x-ray in hand, asking for my son's medical records so I could transfer to another practice. This particular pediatrician took the time to sit me down, warning me that I needed to calm down. I had become obsessed with my child's wellbeing, he explained, to the point that I had become a "hypersensitive, over-reactive, over-protective mother." The fact that my son had been misdiagnosed for five days meant nothing to this jackass egocentric chauvinist. When he finished, I took in a long, slow, deep breath.

"You're right. That's exactly what I have done. And I will continue to be hyper-sensitive, over-reactive and over-protective if that's what it takes to keep our son alive!" I yelled it. I stormed out of the office taking our son's x-rays and medical records with me.

I found my voice. It was easier to accept invisibility when it was just me. But when the physicians tried to ignore our son's health and my pleas, I would not be ignored. I knew to my core I was right and I was no longer willing to take any chances endangering our child.

Within a month, I was back at Children's Hospital in the Pulmonary Department giving Stephen's full history. This physician worked with other TEF children. She listened to me, validated my anger, and addressed my concerns. She kept Stephen's recurrent illnesses to a minimum with aggressive antibiotic treatment and, with daily vigilance, shortened Stephen's illnesses. She developed a treatment protocol that allowed us to maintain Stephen's health for longer periods with nebulizer treatments, respiratory therapy, steroids, and antibiotics. I could do everything at home except IV antibiotics. When we reached that point, we knew the only option was hospitalization. But again, my role as parent was well respected by the entire medical staff at Children's Hospital every single time we were there, starting from his physician and trailing all the way through to the Family Life Specialists and Respiratory Therapists.

Without consciously realizing it, I had chosen to validate my son's pain, advocate for his treatment protocol, and demand only the best from every medical professional who entered his room; something I had wished for as a child. We have always been open with Stephen about his health. I never lied to him about getting a shot; I never lied about having to go to the hospital. I stayed with him 24/7, going home to shower and change only when Jeff arrived with decent food and a new video game.

When Stephen was sick, Jeff or I stayed with him the entire time; something hospitals didn't allow when I was a child. We played games, watched TV, read books together, anything to help take his mind off his illness, even hoping for some healing laughter. I wanted to give my child a very different experience than what I had grown up with. And I was perfectly happy being labeled as hyper-sensitive, over-bearing and over-protective to provide it for him. Besides, I was right.

The Wicked Stepmother

*Rigidity is prevented most of the time as love and compassion
mesh us into tolerant human beings.*—*Kaethe S. Crawford*

Heather and Joey were 10 and 8, respectively, when Jeff and
I married. They came to our home on Tuesdays, Thursdays,
and every other weekend. I didn't know how to be a step-
mother; and with significant tension between "the ex-wife"
and us, I didn't do a very good job the first couple of years. I
was too strict, too rigid, and not compassionate enough. It was
one of those cases of the road to Hell being paved with good
intentions. I wanted the best for Heather and Joey, but I was
going about it the wrong way. And what I thought was best for
them may not have necessarily been the best.

Heather and Joey came to live with Jeff and me a few
months after Stephen was born. The ex-wife agreed making
it a mutual decision among the parents. By then, Heather and
Joey were entering 8th and 5th grades. The Rainey house went
from a house of two to a family of five within a year.

I don't think I made it easy for them; I think my compassion expanded as a result of having Stephen and gaining

a better understanding of children in general. But it was still difficult for everyone.

"I'm going to throw up if I have to eat these green beans," Heather wailed. I still made Heather eat the green beans and drink a glass of milk.

I wouldn't let Joey wear shorts unless it was at least 70 degrees. He snuck them into his backpack and changed at school.

When they complained about the 'right' clothes not being clean when they wanted, I did what my mother did: I taught them how to do their own laundry.

And I definitely didn't hug them enough. It was that awkward state of wanting to hug them, but they were so angry they had a stepmother, and I was in the midst of my own depression. I pulled back instead of diving in.

Eventually, tensions eased with the ex-wife, the kids realized I wasn't leaving, we went through family counseling, and we sort of figured out how to make things work.

Heather works for me now; we have shared an office for almost four years. Heather is now a vegan and loves eating green beans.

Joey gives me great big bear hugs and I send him Marvin the Martian t-shirts.

We each acknowledge that each of us was doing the best we could with what we had. Acceptance and forgiveness have been critical elements of our relationships.

Recently, before I was about to step into a meeting that I knew would be extremely emotional and contentious, Heather texted me a simple message: "Angels are around you."

Time heals even the deepest wounds.

In the Spotlight

With bright faith we act on our potential to transform our suffering and live in a different way.—Sharon Salzberg

As part of the responsibility of being a family, I thought it was important for us to attend church regularly. But because of Robert's abuse, it was difficult for me to fulfill this sense of obligation. Occasionally I could sit through Sunday's service and never give a thought to the transgressions I suffered. And sometimes, I would have to leave early, unable to control my tears.

One particular Sunday, Jeff and I sat in the pews of the church where we had been married. The lay readers were giving the usual weekly readings. A 20-foot high wall of windows illuminates spring's blooming daffodils, flowering fruit trees, and pink azaleas. Skylights invited the morning sun to light the sanctuary as bright as the outdoors.

At no particular point in the service, with nothing specific on my mind, I suddenly felt a burst of warmth against my skin. Suddenly distracted, I looked down at the seat and noticed the pew was lighter and brighter six inches to my left and six inches to my right. I looked up at the skylights, seeing the sun's rays shining through one particular frame directly onto my seat and no one else's. How was I sitting in God's spotlight? Surely there were others more worthy in this crowd; like maybe the rector. As quickly as the question popped into my head, a whiff of cool air whooshed along the back of my neck as though someone had blown a giant, icy air kiss my way.

I turned my head right. Jeff was listening to the readings; no light was shining on him, no cool air had brushed against him. I turned to the left. Stephen was sitting quietly, his tiny legs dangling from the pew. No light was shining on him. He wasn't even looking at me.

A deep, calm male voice clearly enunciated, "My child, you need not suffer anymore." It was not a whisper or a shout. Everyone around me should have heard it.

In the next instant, the brightness disappeared and the temperature returned to normal.

My brain was confused. What just happened? I knew what He said. Was it really Him? No one else around me turned their head. They acted as though nothing had just happened in my seat. No lights, no cool breezes, no words uttered to anyone else. Had the rest of the world momentarily frozen in time as He delivered this message to me?

The message was clear; this one didn't need any interpretation. I had suffered long enough, distortedly thinking that somehow I caused the abuse inflicted on me. I didn't need to think myself responsible anymore; and clearly, with this focused message, a power far greater than myself thought it important enough to stop the world, spotlight me, and clearly and carefully state I should suffer no more. Ok, so time didn't really stop, but I definitely received the message loud and clear.

I definitely heard before the abuse was not my fault, but the rush of the light, the breeze, and the command ushered a quick release of my suffering. The decades of pain, the long-term guilt; they all vanished in the same instant as the command was issued. I was absolved, the shame released.

It's Not Just About the Hair

*One's life has value so long as one attributes value to
the life of others, by means of love, friendship,
indignation and compassion.*—*Simone de Beauvoir*

Even with a healthy marriage and sobriety, my struggle to
connect with others remains a recurring learning opportunity
that God presents to me.

Sometimes, my deepest friendships have come from bizarre
places. My friendship with Jim is no exception.

I saw Jim every month for 17 years. He started his career
as a hair stylist in 1963 (the year I was born). He joked that he
met me when I was young, thin, single, and driving a Mazda
Miata. As life took its twists and turns, he saw me go from a
Miata, then a Minivan, and eventually a Mercedes.

Every month, we caught up on each other's family, raising stepchildren, starting new business ventures, travels, and
politics.

"Whose it gonna be in 2004?" he would ask. His favorite,
Rudolph Giuliani, was always in the top two. "He's Italian, a
New Yorker, and a Republican; the trifecta!"

"Jim, how do you see the South going for an Italian New York?" I retorted. It didn't matter; Jim just wanted to see one of his own make it to the top. He moved on to the other possible party leaders explaining why each didn't have a chance against his favored Rudy.

In the spring and summer, Jim showed me photos of a cabin he built in Canada where he stayed during his annual hunting trips. He fancied himself a remodeler, though he never bothered with 'formalities,' as he called them. He had started his own remodeling business on days he wasn't cutting hair. He complained about not having enough business; I suggested he get his contractor's license.

The cabin was a man's cabin for sure, each room lined with horizontal cedar instead of drywall. He was decorating each room with his grizzly conquests. I am not a fan of hunting for sport, but I looked at the pictures and listened as he led me from room to room, from one kill to another.

We shared our fears and irritations as they arose. Jim was twenty years older, but we were both in the midst of step-parenting and marriages past the first. Sometimes, it became the one ups-man-ship of whose stepchild had done what in an effort to take us to the brink. I liked Jim's bluntness and his honesty. He was by no means politically correct, but everything he said, he believed and felt with a true heart. Even when our children drove us crazy, Jim would pause his cutting shears, rest his hands on my shoulder, lean forward and almost in a whisper, say, "But they're family. And family is what counts the most. We have to love them, you know?" And then he shared about a tender exchange with that same child. And then he went back to cutting my hair. I could envision Jim at one moment in a yelling match with his loved ones and in the next moment pulling them into his arms, professing his love. Jim was Italian all right.

In a city filled with protocol and political correctness, Jim bowed to no one. Jim was authentic, real, whether he was touching up the roots of a Supreme Court justice or trimming the bangs of a 5 year old. His authenticity was refreshing and endearing. My monthly appointments were a non-sexual version of "Same Time, Next Year" with Alan Alda and Ellen Burstyn. We always picked up right where we left off, each changing and growing, yet each visit similar, developing a sense of normalcy.

But one Saturday was not normal. The front desk receptionist told me Jim was in the back and he was not feeling well.

"Would it be all right if someone else does your color and cut today?" she asked. She caught me off guard. I had always arranged my appointments around Jim's and my respective vacations, etc., to the point so in those fifteen years, Jim was the only one who ever touched my hair. I didn't know what to say. I didn't really have a choice.

"That's fine," I finally responded. I glanced around, but didn't see Jim at his chair or walking around.

A few minutes later, Jim walked by while I was sitting at the hair washing station. When he glanced my way, I smiled at him. He did not smile back. His face was swollen and flushed. Beads of sweat dripped as he brushed his arm across his forehead. Had he just thrown up?

I asked, "Did you catch a bit of this flu going around?" This time, my smile was a bit more forced. As each second passed with our eyes looking into one another's, I realized it was not the flu. It was not going to be a simple answer. My gut was already tightening, my own nausea rising inside.

The noise of a busy salon Saturday faded into dullness. The people and objects around me softened in shape and color and brightness. I could see only Jim's face clearly as he sat down next to me. He looked down, took my hand, and looked back up at me with tears streaming down both cheeks. I knew why they were flushed.

Keeping his eyes locked on mine, he said, "I have pancreatic cancer."

I couldn't breathe for a moment. The air had been sucked from my lungs, nothing to feed them, to force them to move and work again. I searched Jim's face to find something would tell me this wasn't true. But it was true.

He gave me just a few brief details, but by then, it was soaking in and tears started falling down my face. This was too hard for both us. He got up, went into the back, and I didn't see him again that day.

Jim fought hard. Some months were better than others. The doctors originally gave him four to six months and he lived almost two years. I was lucky; I never missed an appointment with him. My scheduled dates were when he was well enough to work. Some months he looked pretty good; others, it was obvious the cancer was conquering.

Most of the time, Jim's attitude remained positive and vigilant. We still talked about blended families, shop gossip and politics. He was determined to beat the cancer.

Three months before he died, he hit an emotional low. Our conversation while he worked on my hair was minimal. It had been silent for a while with his face downcast for most of the time. He stopped cutting my hair, looked up at me in the mirror, this time dropping his hands to his side rather than resting them on my shoulders.

"So who is going to do your hair when I'm gone?"

Gulp. I had been wondering the same thing. But I didn't want to say, ""Hey, Jim, when you die, whom do you recommend to do my hair?" I just didn't think it should be one of the questions you ask a dying man. So, instead, I lied, "Now, Jim, I am not even thinking about that. *You* are going to keep doing my hair." His eyes sparkled for a moment, a fraction of his smile returning. For that moment, I outrageously dreamed of a way I could give him the hope he needed to go on for just a while longer. Or was I who needed the hope?

I saw Jim just a few days before Christmas, one of his very last days of work, which neither of us knew at the time. He looked better than he had in months. He was jolly. He was enjoying life again, and not just from the morphine patch on his shoulder. I left that December day thinking, "Hey, he may just beat this . . . ."

Less than a week later, Jim was in the hospital. He died a few weeks later.

It was more than a year before I could go to a stylist and have my hair colored and cut without crying. Every time I looked in the mirror, I thought of Jim. I saw him applying the blond color, cutting my hair, blowing it dry with big, round bristle brushes. I heard him teasing me about politics.

But as time passed, it did get a little easier. My current stylist doesn't discuss politics but she looks at life without a sugar coating. Just like Jim did. When she wants to make a point, she'll stop cutting my hair, rest her hands on my shoulders, and tell me what she thinks. And if I close my eyes, it can sound like Jim whispering in my ear again.

Retreat

She kept secrets--not in drawers or closets or diaries, but in her heart, behind her eyes, on her lips.—Antonya Nelson

More than fifteen years into my sobriety, and almost thirty years after Robert's first predatory kiss, I attended a women's weekend spiritual retreat.

A day into the retreat and a bit frustrated by its absence of divine manifestation, I went down to my room, lay on my bed, and uttered out loud, "Sharon, everything does *not* have to be monumental. You do not have to have a *great* experience. There does not have to be an epiphany. Just take this weekend as it was meant to be and enjoy some quiet time alone. Take this alone time as a gift. It doesn't have to be a huge thing." I took a deep breath. "Acceptance is the answer to all my problems." I needed to accept that it didn't need to be all about me. I could enjoy a restful weekend, getting to know some really nice women. This was the beginning of my *Aha!* moment.

An hour later, I was sitting in a private room in front of Sister Maureen, the retreat leader for the weekend.

"I don't know what we are supposed to do here. I don't even know why I signed up for a time with you," I said. I was uncomfortable, fidgeting on the blue chenille sofa. "But I figured if I was one of the eight people to have private time with you, I better take it. And I'm not even Catholic." I tried to chuckle, valiantly trying to lighten the tension I felt. Full white perm curls covered her head and framed her face. Sister Maureen's fixed expression remained as she relaxed in her seat, her chin raised a bit. She waited, her hands resting on the arms of the chair.

I told her of my struggle since childhood with getting close to other women and maintaining close friendships with them, thus one of my reasons for trying a women's retreat. I related my painful experiences. She told me to schedule coffee weekly with one woman, to just have one-on-one face time with another female. She told me to start taking a course where I could open up with other women and open the possibilities of friendship. She encouraged me to find any opportunities possible to spend more time with other women.

I thanked her for her time and her advice. I started to stand up from the sofa, my face directed towards the door.

And then, almost as an after-thought, I stopped beside her, looked down at her and asked, "And Sister, would you pray for me to find some peace with being in a chapel? I was molested by a minister in my teens; some of the abuse took place in a chapel, so it's hard for me to enter a sanctuary without crying." My acceptance of Robert's abuse had just come forth in a request for help.

I found myself reaching back towards the sofa, grabbing the arm of it to steady myself. Where did that come from? The secret I had kept from everyone (except my husband and psychologist) just came out of my mouth. It was not a topic of conversation for me except on rare occasion in therapy. And yet, the words spilled out with no forethought, no anticipation. Unable to force air back into my lungs, I became breathless. I felt like a Harry Potter "death eater" had just hovered above me and extricated my soul through my mouth. I was tense, light-headed, jarred from a normal discussion into a realm I had no intention of entering until the very second before it happened.

The tears poured quickly, my mind unable to focus on much except for Sister Maureen's words: "My child, he is a sick man . . . you must forgive this man . . . you did not cause this . . . it was not your fault." She repeated these phrases often throughout.

As she said them, she moved forward in her chair, sitting on the edge, nearing me, reaching her hands out to me, just shy of touching me. Her blue eyes softened with empathy, her energy focused on delivering this message of compassion and understanding.

I knew she was right about the forgiveness. The forgiveness is for my sake, not his. If I didn't forgive him, I would never heal. But from my perspective, forgiveness was not my immediate issue; I just wanted to stop weeping every time I entered a chapel. In that thought, my tears subsided long enough for me to notice Sister Maureen's pause, silently looking upward for an extended moment.

"Each time, before you enter a sanctuary, stop," she whispered. Raising her hand up to the sky, she continued, "Look up and say, 'God, I know you have not brought me this far, to this place, only to abandon me now.' In a slight crescendo, she finished, "Lord, take me into your care and heal me.'"

This prayer became both my sign of hope and my action step towards healing and recovery. I still offer this prayer each time before I enter a sanctuary. It is my reminder I am not alone, I am loved by God; thoroughly, unabashedly, and without reservation.

We didn't hug goodbye. I do not even remember leaving Sister Maureen's room. I do remember going back into my room, lying on my bed, and wondering what the heck just happened and why it came out now.

"You asked for an epiphany, kid. Now you got one."

Crossing the Threshold

A crisis is a holy summons to cross a threshold. It involves both a leaving behind and a stepping toward, a separation and an opportunity.—Sue Monk Kidd

During the weekend retreat, each time I crossed the chapel's threshold, I counted it as a victory against my perpetrator. During this retreat, we had chapel three times daily.

During one of these times, the homily was about Gifts from the Sea. I was immediately attracted to this topic as Jeff and I had honeymooned on Captiva Island where Anne Morrow Lindburgh wrote *Gift from the Sea*. One epiphany had already rocked me during the weekend; I hardly expected another. My list of coincidences was quickly growing and it all seemed to be coming together like a giant jigsaw puzzle in motion, creating a beautiful, delicately detailed painting.

Sister June used the pearl as the metaphor in her homily about the gifts. She talked about the pain we endure throughout life and the pain we carry in our souls.

"When a grain of sand, pebble, or parasite enters into an oyster, it becomes a source of discomfort for the oyster," she began. "It aggravates the oyster, yet the mollusk has no way of expelling the sand. It cannot move it around to help ease the discomfort from that one spot."

She paused, offering us an extended moment to recognize our own grains of sand, our moments of pain, trauma, fear; moments early in childhood and moments more recent. For some of us, our hands were not enough to hold the grains of sand; it sifted through our fingers, beyond the palms, pouring to the ground.

Sister June continued, "The oyster must accept that sand, pebble, or organism. But, instead of allowing the intruder to destroy it, the oyster coats it with layers of a solid, slick material called nacre (pronounced NAY-kur). The oyster's mantle tissue secretes the two main components of nacre, cementing the layers together. It coats it again and again to soften the irritation, to ease the discomfort. After years of this process, inside the oyster, we will find a beautiful pearl."

Sister June paused, smiling, giving us the necessary moment to process and discover our own Aha! moment. And this was mine.

What was once the source of pain becomes a precious jewel. The pearl is an exquisite, single gem, formed through the suffering in the heart of an oyster. Most precious stones must be cut, polished and set to reveal their intricate beauty. The pearl, however, is the only gem created from pain and anguish.

With this sand, pebble, or organism, I do not have to analyze why it is there or how it got inside of me. I wasted too many years asking these questions for which there were no answers, and really, no need for answers. What was important at this point was to choose what to do once the trespasser was there. I could allow it to aggravate, redden; I could allow the parasite to sicken me. Or I could coat it with my own nacre, creating the precious gem.

Sister June gave each of us a pearl and encouraged us to carry it with us to remind us of the pain we have carried through our lives. She asked us to take our pain and coat it, over and over. Eventually, she assured us, our pain would become a beautiful jewel.

But what do I coat my pain with? How do I cover the sand without covering up and encapsulating an infection? Somehow, I had to figure out how to coat the pain with something that would allow the core to remain but not infect the rest of it. My nacre needed to be something that would indeed allow it to become that precious jewel. But what? What was the answer to this quantum question? I asked God so many times in my life to take away my pain, my suffering.

In the Bible (Matthew 13:45-46), the parable of the pearl of great price appears. There are numerous analogies associated with this parable but the most commonly accepted is that the Kingdom of Heaven is so great, that man should be gladly willing to give up all his wealth and comfort to obtain it. All heavenly riches are far greater than the sum amount of one's worldly riches. It is about seeking and recognizing the value of God's gift to humanity: his Son. It reminds us the most valuable thing in our life is our relationship to God. I had to take this time to recognize that maybe God was not as silent as I thought He had been. Maybe He had been there, protecting me in ways I could not yet fathom.

Comparing something to a pearl often denotes that it is of great value. In *The Scarlet Letter*, Hester Prynne named her illegitimate daughter Pearl because she had surrendered all she had in giving birth to the child. As a former English teacher, I could appreciate this ironic metaphor for my life experiences. It reminded me again there are no coincidences. The jigsaw puzzle picture of my life was beginning to take shape; pieces were beginning to fit together in order for me to see it all together, as God sees each of us.

Any pain, any grain of sand I carry today will some-day become a pearl. I just have to keep coating it. My *Aha!* moments include, in some form or another, my faith, family and friends as the answer, creating the precious pearls now adorning my neck and the nacre I use to create this beautiful strand of treasured gems.

Taos Tattoo

Out of suffering have emerged the strongest souls; the most massive characters are seared with scars.—Kahlil Gibran

I have a few physical scars that correspond with all too familiar stories of dangerous meetings with kitchen knives and Cuisinart blades, laprascopic knee surgery, torn tendon repairs, and a chance encounter with the oven broiler.

Three scars, each less than half an inch, are remnants of an April morning where, with a tiny slit, the surgeon pulled out over a hundred gallstones a decade in the making. My C-section scar is my largest, proportionate to the drama surrounding the event.

Each tells a story, most of them involving some level of pain; leftovers of trauma survival.

Stephen's 16-inch scar starting at his chest, across his ribs, to his back, usually evokes a compassionate response from the viewer. At birth, the original incision was only two inches. But it has grown as he has. He tells the girls it's a shark bite.

We make allowances for those who bear physical scars; usually likening it to some sort of Red Badge of Courage. The body builds layers of callous to protect itself; to cover the wound and initiate the healing process. The larger or deeper the scar, the longer the healing takes; the more protective layers applied.

Emotional scars are often more difficult to reveal or share; often deeper than any physical wound endured. We can't measure their depth, size or age. We can't surmise how long it took for the wound to heal, or if it has in fact started to heal at all. We can't apply a bandage over the still sensitive area.

Instead, we only see the results of the cicatrix. These emotional scars develop outward manifestations that are, in turn, judged by others on a harsher basis. Because they see only the resulting behaviors, and not the actual scar, they interpret them based on their own experiences and reality; not based on those of the victim.

The cycle begins. Others judge us; then we develop judgments about ourselves. Instead of viewing our scars as remnants from the past, they become a part of our present, in thought, word and deed. The scars from the past affect our present, and thus our future.

"I wish I was more assertive."

"I wish I wasn't afraid of men."

"I wish I could stop drinking."

I don't think I have ever met a person who doesn't have some sort of emotional scar. And yet, we work to keep them hidden, protected; afraid of others' judgments.

We are only as sick as our secrets—I have heard this often in my recovery. Instead of keeping others 'out,' my secrets drained my energy. They consumed me. The wall I was trying so hard to build kept collapsing. The image was merely an illusion that with a single motion could be dissolved. Falsehoods.

Once I revealed the secrets, with another human being, the healing began not just within, but through my thoughts, words, and behaviors.

I thought that I was the only one who:

- was molested by a trusted religious leader;

- wanted to die at age 10;

- grew up thinking the big black hole inside of me would eventually swallow up my soul and kill me;

- thought if they only knew the real me, then they would all reject me and hate me forever.

- married the wrong guy;

- compared my insides with everyone else's outsides;

- the only one who thought, *Is this it? Is this what my life's meaning has evolved as? Is this as good as it gets?*

I was lucky to find out at such a young age (25) there are other people out there who have felt, thought, and done some of the same things I have. I found I never have to be alone again. I found out other people have scars just as large (if not larger), as deep, as riveting, as hurtful, as long lasting, as frightening, as mine. And I found that even though the scars are there, I retain the power to change my life in how I think, what I say, how I act, and what I do.

More importantly, I also realized that my scars are not ME. They do not make me who I am. I still have a choice. This was a critical discernment for me. It was this realization that brought me back to the pearl metaphor. Just as a grit of sand enters an oyster, a trauma occurs to my soul. The grit of sand is forced upon the oyster; the event is forced into my life. But just as the oyster does not become a grain of sand, I do not have to become the traumatic events; someone else's perception does not have to become my reality.

At this point, I have a choice: One, do nothing—whereby the grit will get infected; or two, coat the experience with layers of grace—nacre—transforming the event into a pearl that carries a grit of sand forever at its core. Some pearls take years to form. At least one species of oyster can secrete nacre over an irritant at a rate of about 0.1mm to 0.2mm per year.

My layers of grit-gracing nacre come from a myriad of resources including faith, family, and friends. My nacre has spiritual and emotional elements. Each pearl is different, unique in its shape, color, and luminescence.

In the process of exposing my scars, divulging the conundrums, I discovered a new way of life that now allows me to walk proudly, act humbly, and display my string of pearls with dignity.

The thought of writing this book and its theme evolved during a five-day writers' conference in New Mexico. In an impulsive moment, I walked into the Taos Talisman Tattoo shop, sat down, and asked for a pearl. It was a terrible tattoo. But it was a first step.

Back home, a local tattoo artist created a unique bracelet for my arm. She covered the first mishap and gave me a charmed heart with turquoise-blue mountains. Twelve pearls, representing the 12 Steps of Alcoholics Anonymous, wrap around my wrist.

I spent so many years and so much energy and time trying to hide my scars, the secrets; to hold up an image that was merely an illusion. It was exhausting. This tattoo is not a scar; rather it is a mark of healing. Every day, I see my tattoo and it reminds me of where I want to go, who I want to be.

Reprocessing and Forgiving

Only if you dive for pearls shall you find one.
—Chinese fortune cookie

Another, and maybe the most essential element in creating my pearls, is forgiveness. For me, forgiveness only comes through my faith in God. In creating and establishing healthy relationships with my family and friends, my faith is integral. And anytime we are active in a friendship or any type of relationship, we will always have opportunities for forgiveness. I found myself more able to forgive someone for their actions is when I have been able to reprocess the events with an element of acceptance.

EMDR therapy (Eye Movement, Desensitization & Reprocessing) and Somatic Experience are relatively new forms of psychotherapy. Francine Shapiro, Ph.D, the originator and developer of EMDR, created her technique in 1987. EMDR has been so well researched that it is now recommended as a front line treatment for trauma. EMDR has had a significant positive impact on treatment protocols for patients suffering from Post Traumatic Stress Disorder (PTSD).

In 2008, I started EMDR with a licensed therapist as another means of coating those pesky grains of sand. EMDR therapy is helpful with traumatic episodes in a person's life; it can help with understanding where inhibiting negative thought processes originate and then to reprocess them so they no longer interfere. Let me say that again: it can also help with understanding where inhibiting negative thought processes originate and then to reprocess them so they no longer interfere.

In her 2004 version of EMDR, Shapiro defines trauma as "any event that has had a lasting negative effect." (p. xii). She states, "Large 'T' traumas include natural disasters, combat, accidents, catastrophic illness, rape, molestation, and loss of a loved one. These can result in a diagnosis of PTSD. Small 't' events are those more prevalent experiences that make us feel unsafe, unloved, without control or hop. These can be humiliations, or failures, or losses of any kind (p. xvi)." In other words, EMDR can help with the big things AND the little things.

Shapiro used the example of a patient named Paul. Paul often felt his efforts sabotaged by his belief, "I can't go after and get what I want." He had no memory to explain why he felt this way, only that it was a long lasting belief. During his session with Shapiro, Paul recalled an episode that occurred at age four.

"He was playing with a ball at the top of the stairs. His mother called out to him not to go down the stairs. But the ball fell, and Paul chased after it, then tripped and fell on his arm. His mother came running after him and, grabbing him by the arm, started spanking him for—in Paul's mind—going after what he wanted."

Shapiro clearly states, "Paul's mother was not guilty of abuse. This is the type of experience that children have hundreds of times while growing up. But these types of experiences, just like the big "T" trauma, can take up residence in the mind and govern our behavior for decades."

As I progressed through EMDR therapy, I noted the significant themes in my memories that helped explain my ensuing thoughts and behaviors including silence, invisibility, isolation, and betrayal.

In Somatic Experience, I learned to overcome these hurdles and create a new healthy sense of self. I tried this over the years in talk therapy, but EMDR is *different*. One of my favorite elements of EMDR is I don't have to focus on the pain. It's not about the pain or suffering. It's about the healing. And it doesn't have to be just psychological healing from a past traumatic event.

Recently, I was diagnosed with advanced Lyme disease, requiring me to undergo an extended and complex course of treatment. Intermittently during the treatment, my pain worsened for weeks at a time. It was a deep bone pain that woke me in the middle of the night, sometimes taking my emotions hostage as well as my body. At that point, the fear sometimes crippled me more than the pain.

In EMDR therapy, I reconnected with my 5-year old self in Texas, encountering snow for the first time. I bonded with the energy and the joy as I jumped off my bike and twirled around in the yard. I again felt excitement and joy of a new discovery. I transferred that positive energy to the present. That energy filled my body, shoving the fear out; there was no room for it. I saw myself healed; well. When the current pain increased, reconnecting with that memory was like dipping into an oasis. The anxiety was quenched with hope, anticipation, and excitement.

EMDR is an "action" therapy. I am actually "working" during those 50 minutes. It's not a matter of trying to talk myself into creating a new perspective of an event. In EMDR, I'm actually restructuring my brainwaves, balancing the two sides of my brain.

Another goal of EMDR is to establish a mind/body connection. Often during traumatic events, the victim 'disconnects' from the body in order for the brain to survive the event. This is an important element of survival, but can be detrimental in everyday living.

For months, when the therapist asked me to connect to my body, to get grounded, I had difficulty allowing energy flow or relaxation in my jaw, throat, neck, and shoulders. These areas seemed to have their own filters. The positive energy would not flow there as it could so easily throughout the rest of my body.

In the midst of my EMDR therapy, I heard that Robert, the minister who abused me, was living just 15 minutes from Jeff's favorite fishing hole where we occasionally slip away to for mini-vacations. On one particular excursion, as we drove down the highway, I saw the town's name on a sign. The physical symptoms ripped through me like a tornado. My jaw clenched shut, my neck pulled backward and into my shoulders. My neck muscles were so tight, the right side began to cramp. My shoulders raised, seemingly shortening my neck an inch or two. My back pressed against the seat of the car. My breath was quick and shallow; it hurt to take a deep breath, heaviness thrusting down on my chest. The sunlight stung my eyes. Sweat dampened my shirt. And I remembered the moment when Robert made me do something I had never done before and did not understand until I vomited into my own mouth.

In my next EMDR session, my initial anger, pain and resentment about Robert drained out of me like a punching bag that had been ripped open. I started to feel empty inside.

But through the visualization exercise, I began to re-build my own core.

The core wasn't a grain of sand, either. It was pure steel; steel that filled my bones, solid. I immediately started sitting up straight. It wasn't developing into a coat of armor or protective wall. Rather, the core gave me strength. The steel allowed energy to flow throughout my blood and muscles. It also allowed sadness and grief to travel through, not as a torrent of some storm, but a steady stream that started within and gently flowed out of my hands and feet, exiting without damaging. The black steel turned into a positive white healing energy; tiny, tiny pearls, as fine as pixie dust, sprinkled through every muscle, bone, tendon, ligament, tissue. Each sprinkle healed that part and then spread exponentially restorative to my entire body.

It is now imperative in my day to remain conscious of the tension in my throat, neck, jaw, and shoulders. When they begin to constrict, I stop, reconnect with my body, sprinkle the pearl pixie dust throughout, and reaffirm that I am in control. I decide what happens to my body.

In the midst of this reconnecting mind and body, I also partake in that nagging but necessary act of love: forgiveness. When I reconnect, when I take control back, I must do it with love and not with anger. Anger only feeds trauma. Love and forgiveness release power and control and bring it back to me, for me to choose what happens next.

By no means did this process come quickly or easily. In the Christian best-selling novel, *The Shack,* William Paul Young wrote,

> "You may have to declare your forgiveness a hundred times the first day and the second day, the third day will be less and each day after, until one day you will realize that you have forgiven completely.

> And then one day you will pray for his
> wholeness and give him over to God so
> that God's love will burn from his life
> every vestige of corruption" (page 229).

This declaration of forgiveness becomes part of my reprocessing so it will no longer interfere in my life. Notice that I have changed verb tense here. This is still something I do on a daily basis.

In AA, it's also known as "praying for the bastard." When someone "wrongs" me, in order for ME to gain peace, I must pray to God. I ask God to shower that person with all the gifts and love that God wants for this person.

Notice that I don't pray for what I think this person deserves. If we each got what we deserved, there would be no Grace. And besides, if God showers this person with Grace and love, then it is likely that darkness will no longer settle in this person's soul. For me, evil comes from darkness. If darkness is gone, then the evil will be gone as well.

Throughout my life, I allowed others' negative energy to enter my body and soul and take me hostage. EMDR has taught me how to see oncoming energy and allow it to flow through me without stopping, without taking parts of me, without affecting my core. My favorite picture of this exercise was to spray the other's anger, sort of like using bug spray. It doesn't affect my energy, but it keeps the bugs off.

His Voice

The gift of grace is a manifestation of God's rock solid, faith-
ful, unshakable, unconditional love for us. It is the rock on
which we can build a stable spiritual life.—*Jeff VanVonderen*

I know many people will say they have never heard the voice of God in their lifetimes. I'm not here to argue that point. My purpose here is to simply tell you when I experienced a spiritual awakening so different from any other, so significant, that it became the start of a life change for me. Those are the times when I believe I was given a gift of love, of direction, of grace from my Higher Power whom I choose to call God.

I have heard God's voice five times in my life. The first time was when I was offered cocaine in college. Had I ingested that cocaine, I believe I would have died at an early age from a drug overdose.

The second time I heard His voice was just after I ran outside the house in Okinawa, Japan. That voice saved me, literally and figuratively. It gave me the ability to leave a horrible situation and to start life anew.

The third time was in the church sanctuary, in the spotlight, when I heard, "My child, you need not suffer anymore."

This event led me to realize the fault was not mine; that even though I was a victim at the time, I did not need to be, and should not live my life as a victim.

The last two times I heard God's voice were in New Mexico, within three days of one another. Each was different in purpose. They both occurred on lands that are enchanted and many believe holy.

On a Friday afternoon, Jeff and I were driving through Placitas, just north of Albuquerque. It's a very small community, spread through an area on the Sandia Mountain. The only place we saw other people or another car was at the single building which housed a grocery store, gas station, and the post office. As we drove, six separate rainbows presented themselves to us in less than two hours. Each time, it seemed like we had turned an ON/OFF switch, first seeing only the mountainside landscape and rainstorm clouds, and then brilliant purple, blue, red, orange, yellow arching together. It would shimmer long enough for both Jeff and me to see it, o-h-h and a-w-w over it, and smile together at its majesty. And then it would fade into the landscape as if it was never there.

The scent of recent raindrops still filled the air. Only an occasional hidden bird would chirp. The ground animals had nuzzled away, waiting for the rain to stop completely. At that time, there was no breeze, but the air wasn't stagnant either. There was no cloak of wet humidity; just a fresh feel and fresh scent to everything we saw, felt, heard, and touched.

Neither of us had seen so many rainbows in one month, much less one afternoon. Each rainbow's clear, brilliant colors exhilarated the experience. Towards the end, we even drove through the literal end of a rainbow on the roadway.

We found a small sagebrush meadow at a point on the mountainside. We got out of the car to take in the view, hoping to cement the experience in our hearts. We stood hand in hand

and looked out over the vista, the mountain to our backs. A wind passed through; not enough to chill, but enough to move the fine blond hair on my arms. The breeze lifted a soft lullaby of birds' chorusing. The afternoon had already seemed magical with the rainbows and the scenery. Then, the world stopped.

Our backs were still against the mountain, our view of the vast plateaus in front of us. A soft, gentle whisper, in my ear: "Be still and know that I am here." The words kissed the back of my neck with a soft brush, stronger than a feather, gentler than a paintbrush. I blinked my eyes and turned my head. Yes, Jeff heard it too. We turned towards one another, puzzled by what we each heard.

"Did you just hear something?" I asked.

Taking a soft glance around as though someone might be listening, Jeff replied, "Be still and know . . . ."

"That I am here," we softly chorused.

In a movie, you might imagine some spooky music playing, but on this mountainside, the silence prevailed. Our hands entwined ever more tightly.

We turned our faces back to the west. The sun was setting, painting the landscape every imaginable shade of blue. Layers of purple, brown and orange cut in, dancing over the topography. Then the silent moment faded. As quickly as the moment of His voice had arrived and departed, two wild horses cantered into sight on the adjacent mountain and then galloped back over, out of sight. Those events individually would have been amazing enough, but to put them together in a span of minutes was incomprehensible. And yet, they had occurred exactly that way, in that order in that vastness and in that depth.

Just a few days later, I would hear God's voice another time.

When My Soul Touched God's Heart

God's healing is not just something He does for us; it's something He does through and with us.—Marianne Williamson

A few days after our Friday mountainside excursion, Jeff and I visited White Sands, my first visit since that memory of my early childhood. On this particular early morning, it was quiet, cool and still. There were no birds singing, no cars or people in sight, nothing but the white sand built against the brilliant azure blue sky. The dunes were white, cream, ecru and every shade between—white sand everywhere. Every direction was a breathtaking vista of white sand. Far away, faded into the background, beyond the white sand and dunes, laid miles of mountains.

Waves of white rolled along the hillsides, formed by yesterday's wind. They stood 20 feet and higher, gently ebbing and flowing into one another, softly whispering to their neighbors.

We drove less than half way around the path, parked, and started walking in the flat, open area. The ground was cool, dotted with unusually lingering puddles from a rain the night before. The air was cool too, the sun not yet having the chance to seep through the layers. All was still—peaceful, silent.

The quiet wrapped me in peace. In two directions, white billowing clouds whisked along the sky. Each direction I turned, I saw a majestic view filled with shades of white from the sand clouds and blue from the sky. Slowly, I turned in circles, uncertain where to land my eyes or feet. I could not collect enough of the scenery to hold into in my eyes, my hands, or my body. I wanted to fill myself with this feast of sight, sound, and feel.

At one instant, as I sat relishing God's majestic banquet, I became transported back to that 5-year old child in my front yard, twirling around, amazed, astounded by the beauty of the snowflakes in the desert. I again felt the droplets on my skin, the cool ground beneath my feet. Was I here or was I there?

The white of the dunes spiraled upward, creating a vortex around my body. The blue sky disappeared, replaced with warm, radiant brightness. The energy cocooned me, separating me from the white sand and the rest of the world. Tears began falling down my face.

I sobbed. I wept. Since they came from such a deep place, I wondered if these were tears of pain. I felt even deeper down inside and realized it was not pain, but something very, very different. I did not want to let go.

This fifth time, God's words came to me in His touch. In times before, as gently as the voice had whispered within me, as clearly as it had instructed me, as warmly as it had released my pain, as lovingly as it had kissed me in stillness; this time, I heard, I understood an unintelligible language of love and acceptance and joy.

I accept you . . . . You are my child . . . . I love you.

I accepted God's undeserving grace in His omniscient gentleness and love.

I had hoped and searched, longing for this moment for decades. My constant conversations with God, my questions, my doubts, my struggles, my efforts, all culminated into this single instant of a profound spiritual awakening.

Relieving my heart of all heaviness and burden, God's touch released my pain; it tendered me innocent. The pain and sorrow I carried was coated with grace and healing. God's touch offered me a glimpse of complete joy, wonder and awe—and more.

It was in this moment that my soul touched God's heart; I felt His gift to me; His gift to my soul.

These mountains of white sand swathed my heart and my soul since the first minutes of my arrival. Memories of my first visit to these dunes flooded back, visions of rolling down white dunes, laughing, living; of seeing my mother's smile and feeling her love for me.

I found my pearls in a place where billions of grains of sand are found, in a place where the first atomic bomb was tested; in a place that most people consider desolate and unforgiving. My journey ended exactly where it had begun: in the desert.

"I don't want to leave." I kept repeating in my head. I felt like a child being separated from her mother. I had just been held in the arms of God; I simply could not leave so soon.

Five or ten minutes earlier, I was fine. I had resembled a normal human being, traveling to a popular national monument. And now, my lungs wouldn't expand enough for a full breath. I couldn't swallow past the lump in my throat.

"I don't want to leave."

The tears welled up like an overfilled glass, overflowing in a continuous stream.

"I can't stand not knowing when I will return. I have to come back. I have to come back. I have to be here again. I have to see this again, to soak it in, to feel what I might have missed before. I have to fill the crevices of my brain with these vistas, these mountains, these mesas, these sunsets, these deserts."

There was no reply. Our conversation had closed for now. It was time to leave.

And besides, Jeff quietly reminded me, "We have less than a quarter tank of gas."

I left White Sands that Sunday morning with very little gasoline and an immeasurable compulsion to return as often as I could to this Land of Enchantment.

I know I can hear the Voice of God at any time or place that He sees fit. But the desert is the home of my soul. It is where my cells regenerate, where my heart heals. I feel a part of this land; akin to it. Every molecule of my body feels a part of it. It is where God nurtures my soul, where my ears and my heart open to the truth of life, of death, of forgiveness, and of everything in between.

In the desert, now, I know I am never alone, never invisible. In the desert, I know my voice is always heard.

Family Visit

It seems to me that a pearl of a day like this, when the blossoms are out and the winds don't know where to blow from next for sheer crazy delight must be pretty near as good as heaven.—Lucy Maud Montgomery

We returned to White Sands a year later with Stephen, then 14. I knew not to expect such a strong, visceral experience. I didn't plan to have a repeat. But I was excited to share this sanctuary with him.

Ok, maybe I had a really deep hope that I might experience something that was at least a fraction of what I felt the year before . . . but reasonably speaking, I knew to expect nothing.

This time, we stopped in the heart of the dunes, many families surrounding us, most with young children sliding down the steep hills on candy red and banana yellow sleds and saucers. Giggles and excited screams reverberated in all directions. It was mid morning but not yet hot.

It did not take me long to reach the top of one of the dunes, still at least twenty feet high. For most of the way the path was hard; unforgiving of my footprints. Only during the top third of the way did it allay like a dry, sandy beach. But this sand was fine and soft with glistening white sparkles. The sparkles don't turn silver in the sunlight; rather, they remain white, placid in texture and sight.

Stephen buried his feet, laughing at how it chilled them just with digging a few inches. The heat had not yet penetrated, enabling us to sit atop the mountain for an hour and remain cool by just burying our hands and feet. Jeff brought the camera, helping capture the vistas. He visited the nature center below so he could answer all my questions (What plants are those? How often does it rain here? What's the average temperature?)

For this trip, I had fantasized sitting at the top and tapping the keys on my laptop for a few hours. My poor planning left the white laptop back at the condo. Realizing I was without it, I decided God had another plan for this visit. I needed to be open to what that plan was. So I sat, gazed at the San Andres Mountains, and watched the children run, giggle, scream, play King of the Hill, racing down the hills on brightly colored plastic sleds. I enjoyed the time alone, watching Stephen run up and down the hills, sitting alone himself and soaking in the scenery. I listened to the breeze accented by the children's chatter. I knew I was Home again. This place remembered me. It had waited for me so that I could see it with new eyes all over again; but I did not hear God speak to me.

I recalled my early childhood visit, climbing up the hot sandy hill with my two older sisters, then falling, and rolling down the long incline, laughing loudly, without reservation; my mother watching us, smiling and laughing

I took my cell phone from my pants pocket, dialing my parents. It was still early afternoon in Virginia.

"Hello?" Dad answered.

"Guess where I am?" not even mentioning who was calling.

Chuckling, he surmised, "White Sands?"

"Yep. I'm sitting at the top of one of the dunes, looking straight at the San Andres Mountains towards Las Cruces."

"Do you see the organ pipes?" Mom asked. My phone call had wakened her from an afternoon nap. Obviously, she was still groggy. She had picked up the other extension in enough time to hear my voice and know where I was.

"I think it's the Organ Mountains, hon." Dad replied in his soft southern drawl that I only hear when he has imbibed more than two glasses of wine or, like this time, when he is feeling nostalgic.

"Yep. I can see everything. It's beautiful."

With almost an inaudible sign of reverence, he replied, "Yes. Yes it is."

A Word After

I started this book only knowing I wanted to write a book about healing. I realize now that the part of my life needed to finish the book had not yet occurred. Much of what I have written was learned along the way, in the process. Man, was it painful sometimes.

During the journey of writing this book, I was diagnosed with advanced, chronic Lyme disease, which I believe I have had since the age of 18. My symptoms increased significantly in the middle of this project. I had seen dozens of physicians for a myriad of ever moving symptoms, no one ever even mentioning Lyme.

When my uncle heard my symptoms and a few test results, he said, "I think you have Lyme disease. Please see a Lyme Literate Medical Doctor (LLMD) and get the Western Blot blood test from Igenex lab in San Diego, CA." I listened to Troup because seven years earlier, his wife (my Aunt Betty) died of complications from Lyme disease that was diagnosed and treated too late.

As I wrote this book, I applied what I learned in dealing with this disease and the havoc it wreaked on my body, my emotions, my relationships, and my experiences. I had a fresh format for implementing my philosophy of making a pearl when all I had before me was grit.

I am handing in my final manuscript almost a year to the day after my Lyme disease diagnosis, ten months after our son's Lyme diagnosis, and nine months after Jeff's diagnosis. Yes, all three of us have advanced chronic Lyme disease.

Each month of writing, fleshing out chapters, and editing was accompanied by deep bone pain, extreme fatigue, joint swelling, missed work and schooldays, canceled lunches with friends, lonely nights of despair, and intense treatment. I questioned my ability to write this book because at times, there seemed to be a whole lot more grit than pearls surrounding me.

And then, as it had happened before, in my most desperate, fearful moments, I heard a quiet, calm, clear voice saying, "You *are* healing. You *will* conquer this disease."

My parents, my family, and friends lovingly supported us, unconditionally and unendingly. Jeff, Stephen and I banded together and commiserated about medication alarms, diarrhea, going gluten free, and orange pee. We made our pearls.

As this book goes to print, Jeff, Stephen, and I are still in treatment. And we are all healing, feeling significantly better than a year ago. We are aiming for nothing short of a complete cure.

This project brought significant healing to me. I hope my story brings healing to the reader as well and courage to reveal their own secrets and start the process of acceptance, hope, and action; and hopefully some forgiveness as well.

Most of all, I hope my story illustrates how each of us can create our own beautiful string of pearls even when it seems like the only thing within us is grit.

Acknowledgements

to express appreciation or gratitude for

Nichole Rodriguez started it all with a single grain of sand; **Sister June** made it into the pearl; **Cathy Jaggars** planted the seed; **Jesse Lee Kercheval**—saw the possibilities, and reminded me to "consider the source;" **Scoop**—the first to hear <u>all</u> the secrets, my failures, my pain; you showed me my self-worth, restored my faith, and reminded me how to set myself free; **Kathy Pesavento**—found my treasures; **David Hazard**—editor, manager, comic relief, inspiration, steadfast friend, teacher, therapist, but most of all, supreme among writing mentors, and faithful fan; **Janet Jameson**—guardian angel of mine; **Sherri Krohl**—willingness to be the teacher and courage to be a student; **Kathleen Murphy**—appreciated organizational and editing skills; **Jane Annunziata**—through thick and thin; **Kathryn Ford**—giving me the most integrated, grounded, creative, visual, colorful, present and future I could create; **Anne Loehr**—showing me how to create the big picture with an outline to guide me; **Chuck Cascio**—objectivity, rewriting, respect for authors, integrity, a job well done, a sense of humor when I rubbed your Bic pen in jalepeno oil, and forgiveness when we toilet-papered your Porsche; **Richard Hasker**—teaching Shakespeare so we understood and respected him; for your passion for literature, your skill at teaching writing; **Cindy Waters Dodge** –for your honesty, grace, clarity, and willingness; to the **myNeighborsNetwork. com members** who read my personal blog and said, "You really need to write a book. This is good stuff." This book would never have come to fruition without your encouragement; **Dr. Kurt Newman**—for saving our son's life with your God given talent; **Dr. Hollis Chaney**—for keeping our son alive, believing in us; **Reverend Bob Friend**—acceptance, compassion and trust; **MB**—perseverance, tenacity, hope, humility, and mystery; **Reuben Jackson**—for showing me how to find the poetry of a scene, three lines at a time; **to my fellow Lymies**—gut level determination, courage, and hope. You are a group of true bad-asses; **BRMMD**—you gave me my life back, and my family's life back, putting "the lime in the coconut," one day at a time; thank you for insisting that I aim for no less than a complete cure; **Mom and Dad**—who made everything good in my life possible, and then helped it come to fruition. I will never be able to show enough gratitude for all the gifts you have given me. But I will keep trying!